Which Of Us Are Aryans?

Which Of Us Are Aryans?

RETHINKING THE CONCEPT OF OUR ORIGINS

ROMILA THAPAR
MICHAEL WITZEL
JAYA MENON
KAI FRIESE
RAZIB KHAN

ALEPH

ALEPH

ALEPH BOOK COMPANY
An independent publishing firm
promoted by *Rupa Publications India*

First published in India in 2019
by Aleph Book Company
7/16 Ansari Road, Daryaganj
New Delhi 110 002

This anthology copyright © Aleph Book Company 2019

'The Search for the "Aryan"' and 'Multiple Theories About
the "Aryan"' copyright © Romila Thapar 2019
'The Flight of the Falcon: Early "Aryans" Within and Outside
India' copyright © Michael Witzel 2019
'In the Aftermath of the Harappan Period (c. 2000–500 BCE)'
copyright © Jaya Menon 2019
'The Complications of Genetics' by Kai Friese copyright ©
India Today. Used by permission of *India Today* 2019
'Genetic Origins of Indo–Aryans' copyright © Razib Khan
2019

ISBN: 978-93-88292-38-2

1 3 5 7 9 10 8 6 4 2

Printed at Replika Press Pvt. Ltd, India.

CONTENTS

Foreword: The Search for the 'Aryan'　　　　　　vii
　ROMILA THAPAR

Beyond the Flight of the Falcon:
Early 'Aryans' Within and Outside India　　　　　1
　MICHAEL WITZEL

Multiple Theories about the 'Aryan'　　　　　　30
　ROMILA THAPAR

In the Aftermath of the Harappan Period
(*c.* 2000–500 BCE)　　　　　　　　　　　94
　JAYA MENON

The Complications of Genetics　　　　　　　119
　KAI FRIESE

Genetic Origins of Indo–Aryans　　　　　　135
　RAZIB KHAN

Afterword　　　　　　　　　　　　　　155
　ROMILA THAPAR
Acknowledgements　　　　　　　　　　179
Notes on the Contributors　　　　　　　　181
Bibliography & Further Reading　　　　　　183
Index　　　　　　　　　　　　　　　205

FOREWORD:
THE SEARCH FOR THE 'ARYAN'

ROMILA THAPAR

Since the time when an entity called 'Aryan' was first referred to, a couple of centuries ago, the problems about its definition have continued. Whether it was defined as a label for a language or for a people, the problems grew because in both cases it was assumed that the primary historical requirement was to establish firmly the location and the origin. The search began. Although the word 'Airiia' was known to Old Iranian texts and 'Arya' to the earliest Indo–Aryan texts, these terms were not at the forefront of history in subsequent centuries. As qualifiers, these words were used for those that were respected in society. In the Indian case the word had a broader cultural meaning incorporating a high status. But even as an honorific it was used for those following divergent patterns of life. If the Brahmana was addressed as Arya, so was the Buddhist monk, each within his own community, even if the two were opposed in their beliefs and activities.

In the variant uses of the term, primacy was given to the language that was used, and initially language was the identifier of the Arya. The non-Aryas were the ones who spoke incorrectly and were made fun of, as when described as Mridhra-vac or Mleccha. The Mleccha in later times acquired additional meanings that referred to people of low caste or to aliens. In the nineteenth century, it was thought by some that those speaking the same language belonged to the same race or people. So Arya came to be used for particular peoples. This, not unexpectedly, resulted in much confusion with language and race being used interchangeably. Further confusion resulted with Aryan being the qualifier for other aspects of cultural patterns.

Some clarification about the term Aryan has come from historiography attempting to point out various changes of meaning in their historical context, particularly in recent debates on how it has been used in varying social situations and the change in the usage. The term has its own history of change and cannot be used with the same single meaning throughout the centuries.

Another kind of research stems from not just the reading of the texts alone but with recourse to help from disciplines that can illumine the period with new sources or with providing new meanings for old sources. Nineteenth century studies focused on language and philology, basic to investigating the Vedic corpus. Comparative mythology sought parallels with other societies of Indo–European descent. This meant reading symbols, relating them to cultures and figuring out earlier myths from later myths whilst examining the possibility of borrowed narratives. Reading astronomical information into some sections of the Vedas, suggested a chronological pattern different from that based on philology.

In the twentieth century new evidence came from the approach to the texts through linguistics. It explored forms and meanings as well as possible connections with other languages related in some way. Added to this were more intensive archaeological excavations in the geographical area of the texts that could suggest possible contours of chronology. Some initial reconstructions were also made using the material culture from excavated sites, to reconstruct the kinds of societies suggested by the archaeological data. These reconstructions could then be compared where possible with descriptions in the texts. Suggested reconstructions could draw on concepts from social anthropology.

Historiographical studies of how the texts had been read and were continuing to be read, sharpened the debate. The role of the concept in contemporary politics was recognized as well as its being distinct from the reconstruction that historians were making of that period. This resulted in the bifurcation of the concept into its function as a political symbol as distinct from its being a subject of historical analysis in the narrative of the historical past. The distinction is clear and well demarcated. It is reflected in the writings of those who reconstruct history by using historical methods of enquiry as much as they can, and others for whom it is virtually a play on fantasy.

In studying the Vedic texts, knowing the language in which they are written is the first step. There is a difference however between what is called Vedic Sanskrit and Classical Sanskrit. Fewer people are specialists in Vedic Sanskrit although it was a significant part of philological studies. But now even knowing Vedic Sanskrit is not altogether sufficient. Familiarity with the methods of linguistics allows of a far greater knowledge of the language and of both the history and context of words. This is important to the analyses of words and to the making of connections with other languages, especially where the main sources remain ritual and literary texts.

Very recently, there have been studies from genetics and the analyses of DNA patterns towards mapping populations for this period. These are still being debated. This is different from what used to be called 'race science'. It is concerned with population composition and movements and not with different physical features and the grading of societies as civilized or primitive, advanced or backward according to race. Reliable evidence on population movements, migrations and contacts, mapped as accurately as possible would add considerably to history. It would be better to keep to the genetic labels—at least in the early stages of research—and not impose on them the labels from language or other identities.

When it comes to the geographical areas occupied by those who spoke Aryan languages, we have to erase modern boundaries and think more in terms of geomorphology. The initial geographical frame goes from north-eastern Iran, eastern Afghanistan, the borderlands to Punjab and the Doab. The spread from here is towards the Ganga plain, eventually continuing southwards as well, as far as the Vindhyas and later into the peninsula.

The standard chronology of what is called the Vedic period is taken to be from roughly 1500 to 500 BCE. This is the period of the composition of the first Veda, the *Rig Veda*, and then the later ones, the *Samaveda, Yajurveda* and finally the *Atharvaveda*. It is also the period of the compositions that were exegeses on the ritual texts, such as the *Brahmanas* and the *Shrauta-sutras*. Towards the end of this period came the *Aranyakas* and the *Upanishads*.

In the search for the Aryan-language speakers much has overtaken the initial attempts to provide a viable history. The history of this period has become central to a political ideology that insists on the Aryan culture of the Vedas being the foundational culture of India, and of the Aryans therefore being entirely indigenous to the subcontinent and its earliest inhabitants. This is being projected as the popular explanation of how it all began, especially in northern India. However, it tends to be set aside by most historians. Origins and identities are investigated, but these are not questions avidly chased by scholars. What is being discussed much more now is that insofar as it is a language label how did this language come to be dominant in the first millennium CE, and what were the social changes that took place in this millennium. This involves investigating the structures of societies in different areas and enquiring into how and why they changed.

The concept of the Aryans has been a contentious historical subject as it has been used in various ways to suit a variety of ideologies. What is sometimes called 'the Aryan Question' is probably the most complex question in early Indian history and it requires considerable expertise in the interpretation of the evidence which ranges from ecology to philology to genetics. The basic expertise requires some familiarity with many fields of enquiry: historiography, archaeology, linguistics, comparative mythology, social anthropology and more recently, genetics. The evidence from these when interrelated provides some historical hypotheses. Historians today map cultures, observe their varied interconnections at different levels of society and try to understand the societies that emerge. That there is continual fresh evidence from archaeology, linguistics and other sources further complicates the analyses.

Historiography has now become preliminary to most historical studies as it introduces the intellectual context which shapes historical generalizations. It relates to the concepts with which historians work, their ideological roots and their role in explaining and understanding the past. This is particularly significant when a subject is controversial and where ideological concerns can colour a reading of the evidence.

The discussion of the Aryan in India is an appropriate example. There was a time when language and/or race were primary in defining 'the Aryan'. Now linguistics is important to the definition. For some, the focus has shifted to whether the Aryans were alien or indigenous. Most scholars prefer to focus on the more relevant question of what is meant by 'Aryan' rather than who were 'the Aryans'. This involves analysing whether it was a kind of cultural package that was imposed on an existing population when those that brought it settled amidst them, and this monolith then became foundational to Indian civilization; or, whether cultural elements came in with small circuits of migrants who settled amidst existing cultures and new cultural forms gradually evolved from the interaction of the two. The evidence is substantially of two kinds: archaeological and linguistic. Very recently the results of DNA analyses are beginning to be introduced, their reception being debated.

Archaeological data for this period and subject is extensive. It is to be found in post-Harappan cultures especially those of Punjab and the Doab, the Indo–Iranian borderlands, the Oxus plain and north-eastern Iran. Subsequently the picture from northern India becomes relevant. Coping with fresh evidence from such a large area makes further demands on organizing the argument. The earlier approach of selecting an item from an excavation and trying to identify it with an object mentioned in literary sources no longer suffices. Comparisons between societies as a whole are more valid when seen as a system rather than as reflected in individual artefacts. This involves juxtaposing a combination of items that go into the making of a culture whether they come from archaeology or from a text. Thus, where a cluster of items are mentioned in the *Rig Veda* such as horses, chariots, cattle-herding and the rituals of sacrifice, the archaeological counterpart of such a cluster is sought from the excavations of specific cultures. Such artefacts are not just items in a list of material goods; they provide clues to the structure of the society that they refer to.

Much the same applies to the method of linguistics. In terms of nineteenth century philology it was possible to suggest connections and language identities by resorting to similarities in words from different languages. But the discipline of linguistics requires that the word be placed in the larger syntactic context. This is particularly important, for example, when attempts are being made to decipher the Indus script by applying known languages. Linguistic evidence for this period can come from a variety of languages; the Indo–Aryan of the Vedic corpus and its earliest composition, the *Rig Veda*, and possibly other languages in its neighbourhood such as Dravidian and Munda. Comparative data for Indo–Aryan is available in the Iranian *Avesta* and from scattered fragments of Proto-Indo–Aryan in Anatolia. Familiarity with the linguistic evidence is again quite demanding. In addition, there has to be an understanding of the contents of texts, keeping in mind that Vedic Sanskrit is a specialized form of Sanskrit and not every Sanskritist has expertise in it.

Social anthropology is a more recent addition to the agenda of both the archaeologist and the historian. It can provide a comparative analysis to explain how various societies function. The idea is not to import a model from anthropology or from ethno-archaeology and apply it to the data, but to enquire into the type of questions that social anthropologists ask of various categories of pre-modern societies, and then ask similar questions, where feasible, of the archaeological and historical data. Let me in passing mention one interesting comparison of this sort. The anthropologist E. E. Evans-Pritchard worked on the Nuer society, a cattle-keeping society of Sudan.[1] Bruce Lincoln made a comparative study of this material with the data from

---

[1] E. E. Evans-Pritchard, *The Nuer*, Oxford: Clarendon Press, 1940; *Nuer Religion*, Oxford: Clarendon Press, 1956.

the *Rig Veda* and the *Avesta*, all cattle-keeping societies.[2] It has been the subject of contention but the discussion has resulted in some useful insights into the functioning of such societies. This was also what D. D. Kosambi emphasized in the concept of a living prehistory in India—that there are earlier social forms existing in remoter areas and historians should study these.[3]

In discussing the concept of the Aryan, a fundamental question relates to the spread of the Indo–Aryan language. How does a language spread among people who are speaking other languages at the same time? And together with the spread of a language there are many other items of culture that are also mutually appropriated. It was earlier argued that conquest and warfare brought about the acceptance of the language of the victorious by those conquered. But even where there were no conquests, languages are known to have gradually changed.

Historians look to factors such as a change in society and economy, a social evolution, possibly accompanied by the introduction of new technologies, and the propagation of new rituals. The relevant questions then would be that given that the Rigvedic society was an agro-pastoral society how did it relate to similar local societies or to societies of cultivators? Were they all clan-based societies with chiefs as their authority, in which case similarities would have made

---

[2]B. Lincoln, *Priests, Warriors and Cattle*, Berkeley: University of California Press, 1980.
[3]D. D. Kosambi, *The Culture and Civilisation of Ancient India in its Historical Outline*, London: Oxford University Press, 1965, pp. 40-52.

interrelations easier? What was the social and economic impact of new and more effective technologies of transport and communication such as the horse and the chariot, and the later use of iron artefacts, a metal superior to copper-bronze. It becomes necessary to establish not only when such new technologies were introduced but how they altered society. Rituals can have a dramatic effect as doubtless the Vedic yajnas did in the ambience of what were rather small settlements of the time. Claims to magic and the supernatural would have furthered the effect.

Knowledge requires the teasing out of complexities and this cannot be done by insisting on the answer to a question being either this or that—what I like to call the one-bite answer that the media has now made so fashionable. Often, it is the nuances that lie in between the options that push ideas forward and encourage explanations. This book, therefore, does not claim to provide definitive answers but rather to lay out the field as it were, explain where we are at and indicate by implication the directions in which the analyses could proceed.

BEYOND THE FLIGHT OF THE FALCON: EARLY 'ARYANS' WITHIN AND OUTSIDE INDIA

MICHAEL WITZEL

The question of the origin and the presence in India of the so-called Aryans must be approached by combining data from archaeology, linguistics, population genetics, as well from early Vedic texts dealing with religion, mythology and rituals. They have to be examined critically, by interdisciplinary dialogue, and areas of overlap of data have to be established. Here, an overview is presented that tends to indicate a western Central Asian origin near the Urals with subsequent migration of Indo–Aryan speaking bands, via the Inner Asian Mountain belt and Bactria into India, a process accompanied by acculturation with previous populations, their languages and cultures.

The title refers to the Vedic and Avestan designation of the Hindu Kush Mountains: *upariśyena/upairi.saēna*. It suggests the path of the migration of some Indo–Iranian tribes into Eastern Iran and, subsequently, into Northern India.

To arrive at a comprehensive account of the earliest stages of 'Aryan' (Vedic) India we have to survey data from the Greater Punjab, Old Iran and adjoining Central Asia by triangulating linguistic, textual, archaeological, (ancient) genetic data, supplemented by mythological data (Witzel, 2012). Collaboration between these various fields/

sciences is required but still rare (Harvard Round Tables
1999–2010). Generally, we tend to take over the *results* of
one field, without knowing how such results have been
arrived at, and how (more or less) tentative they may be.
Constant interdisciplinary conversation and countercheck
are required.

The term 'Aryan' is the self-designation of Iranians[1] and
Northern Indians—whatever the etymology (Mayrhofer,
1974). The Persian king Darius (519 BCE) wrote in one of
his inscriptions: 'I am the first to write in *ariya*.'[2] It is not
a 'racial' term, nor strictly speaking, even a linguistic one,
though commonly used by linguists for the early stages of
Vedic Sanskrit, Old Persian, and Avestan: they refer to the
language of the Vedas not as 'Aryan' but as Indo–Aryan.
However, Arya is not used in the Veda to designate the
language of the texts. Only once, Aryavak—'Aryan speech'—
is found in a Brahmana style text (*Kauṣītaki Āraṇyaka*, 8.9),
indicating the area where Vedic Sanskrit was spoken.[3]

A major problem to some extent still is the determination
of the date of the early Arya texts, especially the timeframe of
the *Rig Veda*. Archaeology alone cannot as yet deliver relevant
dates for Northwest India (Greater Punjab). Rather, it is a
combination of textual and linguistic data that indicates the
beginning of the Vedic period. Increasingly, more fine-grained
genetic data may substantiate these results (Witzel, 2001).

---

[1]The name 'Iran' is derived from the genitive plural of *arya*: '*aryānām*,
(the country) of the Aryans.'
[2]Until his time royal inscriptions were in Elamite or Akkadian.
[3]*yatrāryā vāg vadate*, 'where Aryan speech is spoken'.

Here, the data from various sciences will be presented separately, with cross-references indicating overlaps and mutual confirmations, bearing in mind that each field of study has its own particular problems.

ARCHAEOLOGY

After the end of the Indus/Harappan Civilization (*c.*2600–1900 BCE, late Indus period until *c.*1300 BCE), actual 'Vedic' data are hard to come by: the Greater Punjab is overlaid by about 5 metres of alluvium that would cover the thin layers left behind by the semi-nomadic tribes of the Vedic Indo–Aryans. Many interesting areas (in Pakistan, Afghanistan) are little explored and now even inaccessible. In addition, many older (post-Harappan) excavations—in North India, mostly post-1947—are not reported, or badly reported, usually indicating a wide range of old-style stratigraphic and pottery-style arranged data. More recently, C14 dates, now aided by dendrochronology and thermo-luminescence data, provide more accurate dating.

As for a potential beginning of the (Rig)Vedic period, only a very small area of Harappa has been stratigraphically studied, Cemetery H etc., providing data for *c.*1300 BCE. Importantly, while the general Harappan pottery design is maintained, the vessels reveal some new designs and a shift to cremation with subsequent urn burial (Kenoyer, 1998); more recently additional data have emerged, such as the extensive Harappan graveyard at Farmana (Osada et al., 2009; Valentine et al., 2015), and the very recently found burials at Sinauli, of allegedly 2000–1800 BCE, thus in the last stage of the Mature Harappan Civilization. Thus, any overlap between Harappan and Vedic civilizations is not clear yet, though it can be expected for the Haryana/Delhi area.

Importantly, the people of the Vedic civilization were semi-nomadic and its people did not dwell in the post-Harappan agricultural villages of Haryana and its surroundings; instead they were constantly on the move with their cattle (Aryavarta—'the turning around of the Arya').[4] The *Jaiminīya Brahmana* even says that one should *not* stay in a local village, meaning that of 'non-Vedic' people. Yet there was extensive communication (Kenoyer, 2006) between the local sedentary and the pastoral ethnicities. All data from agricultural settlements (Black Red Ware, Painted Grey Ware, Northern Black Polished Ware cultures) should therefore be treated with caution with regard to Vedic people. We still need to find clear pastoral remains of the period, such as in Gujarat and Tajikistan (Meadow and Patel, 1997). However, a recent study of ice core deposits in the western Himalayas correlated with data of monsoon rainfall (Khatayat et al., 2017) indicates that the onset and end of civilizations like the Indus, early Vedic, etc., can be defined by such data. Major changes in monsoon patterns correspond to changes in major cultures: they are now well dated.

Still, it must be pointed out that the Indus/Vedic archaeological data are constantly discussed by revisionist/

---

[4]And take a Kshatriya guide along when travelling there: Then the local (dasyu) people would greet one 'with smiles' (*Jaiminīya Brāhmaṇa*, 2.423).

Hindutva writers, who proceed in the manner of Christian fundamentalists by exploring disagreements between *individual* scholars: this is then taken to indicate that the subject/field would and could not provide reliable results. Instead, they habitually push 'alternative facts' and imagined dates reaching back into the *early* Bronze Age (Kali Yuga, starting on 18 February 3102 BCE) or even beyond, into the Paleolithic.

Examples include, first of all, the question of horses and chariots. Horses, unlike donkeys and onagers, were steppe animals that were imported into the Ancient Near East and early India only around 1900/1700 BCE.[5] Indeed, early Indian horse bones and figurines are attested around 1800 BCE (Meadow, 1983). All (archaeological) reports about 'Indus horses' are spurious (R. Meadow and A. Patel, 1997): skeletons of horses, onagers and donkeys can only be distinguished by their phalanges, but we still do not have good specimen collections.

In fact, in Mesopotamia, the non-Indo–Aryan Zagros mountaineers (Lullubi, Guti, Kassite) and the Mitanni immigrants from the Caucasus area in the north, all moved, during the second millennium BCE, into the Mesopotamian plains with horses and chariots. None of them were Indo–Aryan or Indo–European speaking (Witzel, 2001, 2005), though both groups have many Indo–Aryan loanwords for

---

[5]The Siwalik *Equus* had long died out during the megafaunal extinction *c.*10,000 years ago. Some even bring up the still earlier long-extinct, three-toed *Equus namadicus*.

their horse culture (Mayrhofer, 1974; Balkan, 1954).

Further, 'chariot' implies a lightweight (30 kilogram), horse-drawn vehicle with two spoked wheels, mounted by one or two riders (rathin, rathestha). This is clearly *not* the case in the recent find of 'chariots' at Sinauli that have *full* wheels and will have been drawn by bullocks, like the Harappan toy carts and the massive Daimabad bronze race cart.

The first, still unwieldy proto-chariots (*ratha, its driver: *rathin, *rathaista) were invented in the Ural area (Sintashta) around 2000 BCE, and then imported into the Near East including Egypt in the early to mid-second millennium. Thus, a date for horses and chariots in northwest India is likely by the mid-second millennium BCE. This could overlap with the earliest Vedic texts.

A possibility for the introduction of Indo–Aryan speakers and horses is the Gandhara grave culture (*c*.1600 BCE), for example in Swat with horses, and later with iron. Another candidate would be that of early iron age (Possehl and Gullapalli, 1999) Akra in Bannu, in the western hills of Pakistan that has been dated to *c*.1000 BCE (Magee et al., 2005). It features stone fortresses, like those of the chieftain Śambara in the *Rig Veda* who could not be overcome in his '99 forts' for forty years. This site presents a good overlap between texts and archaeology, which extends to linguistics, as the name Sambara is non-Indo–Aryan.

Clearly, more archaeology is required: we need the excavation of old sites like Akra and others in the hills of Pakistan, in the Indian Himalayan belt (Agrawal, 1998) and in elevated places of the Punjab (like Lahore) that lie well above the ancient flood plain. Ground penetrating satellite data (and drones) may now help to identify even shallow pastoral residential accumulations for future excavations. It has not yet been done.

Further, archaeologists have not yet paid sufficient attention to another path of migration into India, via the mountains of the Tian Shan and Pamir (Witzel, 2004; Frachetti, 2012). Extensive inter-regional pastoralism, from *c.*3000 BCE onward, resulted in a common substrate that extended to neighbouring groups. This mountain corridor provided excellent grazing ground above the tree line for the Indo–Iranians in the areas now occupied by the Turkic Kirgiz herders, all the way from Kirgistan to the Pamirs, Hindu Kush and northernmost Kashmir.

A difficulty remains in establishing the nature of populations that inhabited archaeological sites. The sedentary (post-Indus) farming population in villages and remaining small towns in Haryana etc., has to be distinguished from the hardly attested semi-nomadic Vedic tribes (in constant motion with their animals) that left only shallow accumulations of residue; in addition their settlements had to be burnt down, as the Vedas say, when they moved on to their next grazing grounds: only post holes and a few broken vessels may remain.

Still, pottery remains and linguistic data clearly indicate extensive communication between the two populations: there are many non-Indo–Aryan loanwords from before, during, and after the Rigvedic period.

LINGUISTICS

Comparative historical linguistics is much discussed now by revisionists, though without any penetrating insight into the aims and methods. A brief overview is therefore in order. The comparative and historical linguistic study of Proto-Indo–European emerged in the first decades of the nineteenth century (Bopp, 1816) and has been formalized by the neo-grammarians along strictly scientific lines since the 1870s. This has been done not only for Indo–European but also for several other language families (such as Dravidian or Polynesian) and has been very much refined over the past 200 years. But, the Indo–European and the Indo–Aryan (not 'Aryan') branch of the family has been constantly attacked by revisionists and Hindutva writers as '(colonial) pseudo-science'. Why does linguistics work worldwide, but not in India? This is myopic, and we all know the reason.

Actually, comparative and historical linguistics is a *natural science* as far as the development of the *sounds* of language are concerned; after all, they are produced by the mouth etc., and can accurately be measured scientifically. Though, establishing comparative *meanings* is more complex. For the secure historical development of meanings, we would need a large-scale database and input using artificial intelligence (AI).

Yet, there is the *proof of the pudding*: the sounds of early (Mycenaean) Greek kw and the Hittite laryngeal h2 had been reconstructed (predicted) in the nineteenth century, but they were discovered in writing in newly deciphered texts only in 1916 (Hronzy) and 1948 (Ventris).

Clearly, most of the current North Indian languages and their predecessors (Vedic, Prakrit, Pali etc.,) are Indo–European and are closely related to the other Indo–European languages found from Iceland to Xinjiang (Tocharian), Anatolia (Hittite) and Iran (Avestan, Old Persian, mod. Pashto, etc). Similar reconstructions could be made for the South Indian languages (Dravidian, Ellis, 1816; Caldwell, 1856), and for the Central/East Indian Munda languages, related to Khasi and Nicobar (Austro–Asiatic), as well as for the Tibeto–Burman languages in the Himalayas, Assam and Burma (Tibeto–Burmese).

In addition we have a number of small enclaves of remnant languages: Burushaski in northernmost Pakistan, Kusunda in the hills of Nepal, Nahali in Central India,[6] Vedda in Sri Lanka, Andamanese, and several other languages only appearing as substrates in current languages, such as Masica's 'language X', with many agricultural terms that underlie Hindi,[7] or the Australian residue in Tamil (Blažek, 2006). The field of substrate studies is unfortunately completely neglected in India (Witzel, 1999).

There is thus a long prehistory of Indian languages, for the past 60,000 years. From the beginnings, there has been a multiplicity of linguistic data sets, and never a single, or even dominant, language of ancient South Asia—not even

---

[6]Some 25 per cent of its vocabulary represents the oldest Indian (substrate) vocabulary.

[7]And actually many other Indo–Aryan languages, from Dardic to Marathi.

for the area of the Indus Civilization.

Against this background we can now examine the Indo–Aryan migration path.

While the *Rig Veda* is a South Asian text of the Greater Punjab (as its river names—Sindhu, Krumu, Gomati, Vipas, Yamuna etc.,—amply attest), the speakers of its ancestral Proto-Indo–Iranian language clearly lived in the Russian/Central Asian steppe belt. From there they spread southwards, to Afghanistan (Bactria) and Iran etc., some via the Inner Asian mountain belt (Tian Shan, Pamirs; Witzel, 2000). This is obvious as they have left many loanwords attested in the various Uralic languages, through all their stages from Proto-Uralic to the ancestors of Finnish, Hungarian, Komi, Mari, etc., such as pakas 'Bhaga', Asura, *śata '100',[8]orja 'Aryan slave' *kekra (cakra) 'wheel', *resma (rasmi) 'rope' etc (Rédei, 1986 and 1988; Koivulehto, 2001; Kuz'mina, 2001). The Proto-Indo–Iranian, probably represented by the Sintashta/Andronovo cultures, were at a culturally more developed level than the forest (Taiga) dwelling Uralic tribes. At a later stage, after the apparent departure southwards of the Indo–Aryan (Burrow, 1973), the remaining (Proto-) Iranians supplied an even larger amount of loanwords to the Uralic and Slavic languages, such as Iranian baga> Slavic bogu 'god', Don, Dnyeper, Danube.

The next attestation of Proto-Indo–Iranian words is that of Indo–Aryan words in the Mitanni kingdom (*c.*1600 BCE) of North Mesopotamia, and other contemporary documents:

---

[8]Reconstructed forms are indicated by asterisk (*).

horse colours (at Nuzi in eastern Mitanni); the horse training manual of Kikkuli (fourteenth/fifteenth century); the maryannu chariot fighters,[9] the Mitanni–Hittite agreement (1380 BCE) mentioning the major Vedic gods (Mitra, Varuna, Indra, Nasatya (Asvin), royal and nobility names, attested all the way from Palestine to Nuzi (Diakonoff, 1971).

Incidentally, the Indo–Aryan loanwords in Mitanni confirm the date of the *Rig Veda* for *c*.1200–1000 BCE. The *Rig Veda* is a late Bronze Age text, thus from before 1000 BCE (Possehl and Gullapalli, 1999). However, the Mitanni words have a form of Indo–Aryan that is slightly older than that: they have forms with –az- as in mazda(= mazdhā) that, with post-Mitanni linguistic change, appear as Ved.–e-, in medh-ira (Witzel, 2014); the same sound change is seen in many perfect forms such as sede <*sazdai (Avestan hazde), a development that still is in analogical progress in the *Rig Veda*. Clearly the *RV* cannot be older than *c*.1400, and taking into account a period needed for linguistic change, it may not be much older than *c*.1200 BCE.

The question is how the early Indo–Aryan arrived in the Iranian and Greater Punjab areas. While the archaic Indo–Aryan that influenced the Caucasus-derived Mitanni *may* have come via the plains at the eastern end of the Caucasus, it is more likely that its speakers too had migrated first to Bactria (Witzel, 2003) and from there westward to the Zagros, where they also have left horse-related loanwords in Kassite (Balkan, 1954).

---

[9]At Tell Leilān in northern Syria now even attested shortly before 1761 BCE.

There is a host of 'foreign' loanwords taken up into Indo–Aryan (and Old Iranian, Witzel, 2015) along the path of migration into Uzbekistan/Tajikistan, and from the Inner Asia mountain belt (Witzel, 2004).

By the thirteenth century BCE there is an archaeologically attested transition to mountain cattle-breeding and an increase in riding skills (sparsely attested in the *Rig Veda*) along with active advancement to the south (Kuz'mina, 2007).

The Indo–Aryans basically occupied the same alpine pasturelands as the modern Kirgiz. Importantly, both Indo–Aryan and Avestan know of the *Muza land, attested as the mountain Muzh Tagh Ata/river Muzh Kol in the Kirgiz territories of extreme western Xinjiang and northernmost Kashmir, and as Vedic Mujavant (for the best Soma), Avest. Muža person and land (Witzel, 2004).

It is in these areas that the Proto-Indo–Iranians picked up the new mind-changing drink Soma (aṃśu), and some of the vocabulary connected with its preparation and rituals (Kuiper, 1991).

Other loanwords are due to the interaction with the plains people of the Bactria–Margiana Archaeological Complex (BMAC; Witzel, 1999, 2004, 2015), surprisingly, like Indra, Atharvan/Gandharva/Śarva, ṛṣi, iṣṭa 'brick', uṣṭra 'camel', khara 'donkey', etc., (Lubotsky, 2001). Some data point to an amicable coexistence of the immigrating speakers of Indo–Aryan (with hundreds of attested pastoral sites) and the people of the BMAC urban centres (Kuz'mina, 2007, 284): Andronovo pottery turns up after 1800 BCE.

Coexistence was possible due to separate economic and cultural specialization: the Andronovo Indo–Aryans were semi-settled cattle breeders and suppliers of bronze articles, which they exchanged with BMAC farming products and wheel-made pottery. This contact would account for many BMAC words in Indo–Aryan and even more so in Old Iranian (Witzel, 2015).

There is also some (indirect) influence from the Near East, accompanying the spread of agriculture in the seventh millennium to the borders of India (Pirak), such as godhūma 'wheat' ~ East Iran. gantuma, Caucas. (Proto-Kartvelian) *ghomu, all derived from a Near-Eastern word (*xand); (Witzel, 2004) or the word for 'donkey', khara, Avestan xara.

Further south there are a number of loanwords that go back to Hindu Kush interaction, such as kāca 'crystal', (Hoffmann, 1975–76; Mayrhofer, 1986–2001: 335; Witzel, 1999) or the female Šuci mountain spirits (Kalasha Varōti~ Ved. Apsaras), or the Nāgas that surprisingly are connected in the Nuristani and Dardic areas (including Kashmir) with ice and snow, as well as with lakes, ponds and rivers.

The arrival of the Indo–Aryan speakers in the Greater Punjab is heralded by a host of loanwords derived from the substrate language of this area, the generally neglected Northern Indus language. There are about 300 loanwords in the *Rig Veda* (Kuiper, 1991, Witzel, 1999), even if we subtract the loans that have occurred earlier in the Inner Asian mountains and in the BMAC. Importantly the oldest *Rig Veda* loans are not from (Proto-) Dravidian (Witzel, 1999). I have called this northern Indus language, unfortunately misunderstood, 'Para-Munda' as it shares *only part* of typical Munda traits, the preference for prefixes but not the typical infixes. This substrate exerts a considerable influence on Vedic, for example in unusual sounds (ṣ after a/ā, s after i, u), in word building suffixes (-ūṣa, -īṣa), in the use of the particle iti in quotes, and in the innovative formation of absolutives in -tvā/tvī and –ya); the latter two are not due to Dravidian influence as they are also found in Burushaski and Munda, just as the retroflex sounds (ṭ, ḍ, ṇ, ṣ etc.,), which are most numerous in the Hindu Kush area, where they cross linguistic families: Kalasha, Pashto, Burushaski and Khotanese Saka. This clearly is a regional feature that has influenced all languages that passed through this not yet recognized 'retroflex belt'.

It remains unclear which part of the Indus population spoke the Rigvedic substrate language(s), as the Indo–Aryans took over the loans only after the dissolution of the Harappan civilization, in the later part of the second millennium BCE. The loans indicate, like those in the BMAC, close communication between locals and the newly immigrated Indo–Aryans, especially in the areas of agriculture, plants, wild animals, music/dance, low level spirits and demons (while many Indo–European/Proto-Indo–Iranian designations are retained: for horse, cattle, sheep, dog, certain wild animals like the wolf, beaver; barley and some less favoured cereals, etc.,).

Importantly, the Rigvedic period was characterized by close contact with the non-Indo–Aryan population of the Greater Punjab, resulting in the incorporation of some elements of the local leadership (chieftain Bribu, Balbutha) and even in traditional Proto-Indo–Iranian/Indo–Aryan poetry and poets (Kavasa, Kanva) whose names clearly are non-Indo–Aryan (Witzel, 1999). This comes to a certain halt with the codification of the four classes, varna—Brahmana, Rajanya (Kshatriya), Vaishya and Shudra—in the late Rigvedic period (*RV* 10.90.12).

There are *no* loans reflecting the international trade of the Harappan civilization, their seals, their staple cereal (wheat, that appears only from the *Atharvaveda* onwards), their towns, their mythology (e.g., involving a tree goddess and a tiger etc.,). Clearly, the Rigvedic loans were taken from the post-Harappan rural population. They increase in number in post-Rigvedic times (Witzel, 2006) and involve other language families, including a form of Dravidian, though not (Proto-) Tamil as there are many loans that start with b-, d-, g-, etc.,

In fact, it remains unclear where exactly and since when speakers of Dravidian languages have been present in India (Krishnamurti, 2003). This has been under discussion for more than half a century: did they come from Iran? (Zvelebil, 1970, 1972).

How far do the connections with Uralic lead (Andronov, 1971; Zvelebil, 1972, 1990; Burrow, 1968) or is that a trait shared with other Nostratic languages? A link with the linguistic isolate Elamite has also been proposed (McAlpin, 1975, 1981). More securely, there is a fairly early Dravidian presence in Sindh/Maharashtra, attested in place names (Southworth, 2005, 2006), while the *Rig Veda* and other Vedas do not supply any data for this area. A study of the

Sindhi substrate data should settle this. Curiously, the name of the 'Shudra' (*Rig Veda* 10.90) may go back to a Sindh substratum: Alexander's Greeks (326 BCE) noticed the Sudroi [śūdra] people on the border of Sindh and Punjab. Though not provable, this may be one of the several cases in history where a tribal name was expanded to include a wide range of related tribes.[10] The term Mleccha for 'barbaric' tribes may likewise go back to the population of the lower Indus, the Meluḫḫa people known to the Mesopotamians, cf. Pali 'Milakkhu'.[11] Finally, even older data are found in the Australian language substrate in Tamil (Blažek, 2006), which is due to the migration of Out-of-African populations along the coast, via India to Southeast Asia/Sundaland and to Australia, some 50,000 years ago (Pitchappan, 2008).

GENETICS: DNA AND aDNA

Just as the fields of archaeology and linguistics, the rather new branch of genetics, population genetics, has its inbuilt problems. Earlier data (Cavalli–Sforza, 1994) were based on comparison of modern genetic features, the female-transmitted mtDNA, and male-transmitted Y chromosome data (NRY). These delivered some problematic dates, due to broad error bars found in its early results, just like early archaeological c14 dates did before tree ring correlation. Modern DNA did not allow to distinguish the dates, e.g., that

---

[10]Ionians/Yavana,   Türk/Turuṣka,   Tājika,   Germani,   Francs/Ferinji, Alemanni, Volscae/Welsh, Veneti/Wenden, etc.,

[11] More data will be forthcoming by Witzel for substrates in Sindhi, Punjabi, Tharu, see for now: SARVA substrate dictionary of Indian languages.

going back to an Old Persian official in the Punjab and that derived from a 1200 CE Turkic migrant from Central Asia. Autosomal data points (600,000), reflecting both parents, have helped to refine such data. A revolution has occurred, some ten years or so, with the possibility to sequence ancient DNA (aDNA), which has allowed to specify population history in increasingly fine detail. The future clearly is in aDNA studies. While as late as in 2009 we had no aDNA, now there are some 4,000 samples available.

Unfortunately, aDNA has not yet been extracted from ancient Indian skeletons. Also, the picture derived solely from modern DNA does not (always, or typically) reflect that presented by aDNA: many changes and shifts in population have occurred since. The recent announcement in a newspaper was precocious (Joseph, 2017) though, finally, some DNA from the Harappan civilization at Rakhigarhi has been announced (see below). Just a few months ago, D. Reich (Boston) still told me that we do not yet have workable Indian aDNA, even though that from Petrous bones (in the inner ear) allows for much better genetic preservation in skeletons. The monsoon climate just does not help.

Nevertheless, we could already state (Reich et al., 2009) that India has two ancient strands of anatomically modern humans, that is after the initial settlement out of Africa, *c.*60,000 years ago: the Ancient North Indians/Ancient South Indians (ANI and ASI), not to be confounded with the speakers of the much later Indo–European and Dravidian language families. In general, India mostly is characterized by maternal mtDNA (haplogroup L3 >) M, N > R; and the paternal NRY R1a1 > R2 as well as H, L, J2. The origin of R1 in Central Asia, spreading both to eastern Europe and India, suggests PIE connections (Underhill, 2015).

Haplogroup H seems to be of Indian origin, L and J2 are found spread in the West, from Iran to the northern Fertile Crescent and the Mediterranean, underlining some (non-PIE) western connections, seen also in the spread of agriculture from Iran. After much initial genetic mixing, restrictive marriage rules (intra-caste, extra-gotra) have led to the *codification* of multiple genetic strands over the past 1900 years or so (Moorjani, 2013).

Recent excavations at Indus sites (Farmana cemetery, etc.,) have yielded no genetic results so far. Last year's announcement in an Indian newspaper (Joseph, 2017) of Indian aDNA had not been substantiated as we did not then have aDNA. It merely listed *possibilities*, not results. This has changed as we now (May 2018) have aDNA from the Swat Valley (V. M. Narasimhan et al. 2018).

Further, definite if somewhat vague reports about aDNA from the Harappan site of Rakhigarhi have finally (June 2018) been announced in several newspaper reports (Venkataramakrishnan, 2018). Both are preliminary reports that await publication.

The Rakhigarhi data, published in the *Economic Times* on 13 June 2018 (Vishnoi, 2018), purports to show, in the words of the excavator, V. Shinde, that 'the Rakhigarhi human DNA clearly shows a predominant local element... There is some minor foreign element, which shows some mixing up with a foreign [Iranian] population... This indicates quite clearly, through archaeological data, that the Vedic era that followed was a fully indigenous period with some external contact.' Niraj Rai, the genetic specialist of the soon-to-be-published Rakhigarhi report, echoes this.

Yet, at the same time, Rai sustains Vagheesh Narasimhan's May 2018 paper: 'A migration into [ancient] India did happen... It is clear now more than ever before that people from Central Asia came here and mingled with [local residents]. Most of us, in varying degrees, are all descendants of those people.' Importantly, the R1, a genetic marker, which is typical of the western Central Asian steppes (and Eastern Europe), is missing in the Rakhigarhi sample.

Later newspaper reports add more materials and are much more balanced than the one in *Economic Times* (Bal, 2018; Bhutia, 2018; Venkataramakrishnan, 2018). The initial conclusions about 'no Aryan invasion' echo the cultural politics of the past thirty-odd years and are weird as one cannot expect the genetic materials of Indo–Aryan speakers in the Harappan Civilization: they entered the subcontinent only after its dissolution, or at its very best, during its final phase around 1300 BCE—not more than a thousand years earlier, at the time of the excavated materials, said to be of *c*.2600 BCE.

Even then, some archaeological data had already revealed that the Indus population was not homogeneous and that individuals had moved into Harappa from distant parts of the Greater Indus area (as seen in teeth enamel etc.,). So, just a few months ago the jury still seemed to be out. But, after decades of (originally Soviet–Marxist) denial of *any* migration into India by Indian and American archaeologists, the pendulum is now swinging back to indicate constant contact, migration and population mixture (indicated by gene flow)—which would, at a minimum, *allow* for the migration of Indo–Aryan speakers into the subcontinent.

Precisely this has been maintained in the recent pre-publication of a massive genetic paper by Vagheesh M. Narasimhan et al. (Narasimhan, 2018). According to this study, there is a southward spread of steppe pastoral people to 'Turan' (Bactria, Uzbekistan, Turkmenistan, Tajikistan) from 2300–1500 BCE, for example at Gonur after 2000 BCE, where there also was some mixture with the population of the Indus periphery. There was a limited spread from the BMAC area further south (2100–1900: BMAC graves in Mehrgarh 2100–1900 BCE), there was no further population spread into India.

However, in the late second millennium BCE, a large scale Middle/Late Bronze Age steppe migration entered the Indus periphery, apparently at least in part via the Inner Asian mountain corridor (Frachetti, 2012; Witzel, 2004) where up to 30 per cent steppe DNA is found with the Kalasha in Chitral, in westernmost Pakistan. This movement includes, from 1250 BCE onwards, one to the Swat Valley, where for the first time Indian aDNA has been retrieved (Narasimhan, 2018). Obviously this precisely fits, both in time and space, the migration of the Indo–Aryan speakers of the *Rig Veda*, visible in archaeology and linguistics. These Late Bronze Age migrants have also left a clear imprint on the genetic set-up of the modern Brahmin and Bhumihar population of north

India, where Central Asian traits are up to 57 per cent, while with other populations this amounts only to 11 per cent and is hardly seen in south India.

All of this has a parallel at the western end of the steppes. Central Europe has seen a massive immigration of people with Pontic steppe genes (from the Yamnaya culture of the Ukraine) that overlaid the previous Near Eastern farmer populations (present since *c.*9000 BCE), as well as the original hunter-gatherers from Africa (*c.*40,000 BCE)—with a surprising 75 per cent replacement of aDNA genes (Haak, 2015; Laziridis, 2017). The Pontic immigrants were in all likelihood speakers of a Western Indo–European language, for example, the predecessors of Celtic and Germanic. All of which would be a good model for the Vedic period as well.

RELIGION, MYTHOLOGY, RITUAL

Just as new languages can be acquired within a couple of generations, religion and rituals, too, can be adopted very quickly. Note again, the several clearly non-Indo–Aryan names of prominent poets and 'kings' in the *Rig Veda*: such as the poet Kavasha, and the chieftains Bribu and Balbutha (Kuiper, 1991; Witzel 1999). On the other hand, rituals can also be very archaic. A typical example is the Agnicayana (Atiratra) ritual of Kerala that goes back to *c.*3000 years old Vedic texts, while the religion of the surrounding population is that of modern Hinduism. When comparing the texts on Vedic religion, mythology and ritual with those of the Indus Civilization and of those of the Proto-Indo–Iranian and Indo–European ancestors of Vedic culture, it is clear that the Veda is *not* a continuant of the Indus Civilization (or even an overlap)—with the possible exception of some low-level deities, spirits and demons (kimīdin, mūra-/śiśna-deva) that frequently are isolated linguistically and belong to the Greater Punjab ('Para–Munda') substrate.

The evidence for Indus mythology (visible on small tablets and some seals) is not reflected at all in the Vedas, and the supposed link with later Hinduism, thousands of years later (championed by Parpola, 1994), is a fantasy: for example the famous Śiva Paśupati seal reflects a widespread Northern Eurasian deity, the Stone Age 'Lord of the Animals' (Srinivasan, 1984). Other supposed continuities belong to 'low level' cultural features: the red parting line in married women's hair, and even the namaste gesture, which surprisingly is found in the BMAC at *c.*2000 BCE, and in prehistoric, Jōmon time Japan, in *c.*1900 BCE: certainly not the spread of an Indus feature.

Instead, the Veda contains numerous remnants of Indo–European (and Proto-Indo–Iranian) religion, ritual, which are well known, and thus are merely mentioned here: Father Heaven (dyaus pitā), fire worship (agni), ancestor worship (piṇḍapitṛ) ritual for the three direct ancestors, the Greek Tritopatores; Uṣas, the daughter of heaven (~ Greek 'Eos', Latin 'Aurora', Germanic 'Ostera', 'Easter', etc.); the two sons of heaven (Aśvin, Diskuroi, Castor and Pollux, Hengist and Horsa; Lithuanian Ašvinai). The deity preceding the Vedic/Avestan Indra, and his dragon slaying (~ Herakles/Zeus, Apollo, Sigurd, Thraētaona), are also found in Nuristan data, even in early Japan (Susa.no Wo).

Ancient Indo-European domestic (gr̥hya) rituals for marriage, death, guest worship, etc., are well reflected in Vedic texts, especially in the *Atharvaveda* and in the later codified *Gr̥hya Sūtras*.

The ancient sacred Indo-European drink was fermented honey (mead, Sanskrit madhu, the Greek drink of immortality, ambrosia). Due to western Central Asian influences it has morphed into the bitter Indo-European soma/Avestan haoma drink, most probably pressed out (su) from ephedra. The *Rig Veda* myth about its arrival, carried by an eagle, echoes the Greek one in the ambrosia myth. An elaborate ritual was developed both in Iran and Vedic India for its preparation and use that is still performed by traditional Brahmins, especially in South India (as well as by the Zoroastrians of Yazd/Kerman in Iran and their Parsi brethren in Mumbai); as mentioned, Soma is a Central Asian innovation (Witzel, 2004). Indeed, the best Soma is said in the *Rig Veda* to come from Mt Mūjavant, a striking, high mountain in Southwest Xinjiang, still called Muzh (Tagh Ata), as well as in northernmost Kashmir under the same name (both are Kirgiz areas).

In short, there are many reminiscences of Indo-European and Proto-Indo-Iranian myth, religion and ritual in the Vedas. They have been transported by the speakers of Indo-Iranian to Iran/India, and certainly do not stem from the BMAC or Indus civilizations.

These survivals extend even to some institutions of society. Both the Greek and Vedic divisions of society originally included only the priests/poets (Kavi, Brahman,

Rishi), the nobility (Kshatriya, Rajanya) and 'the people' (viś), but in both cases a fourth class, the śūdra or Pan-Hellenes was added. An important institution was the young men's association, the Männerbund sodality: teenagers had to prove themselves by territorial expansion (landnama), and by some ritual (including the Spartan killing of a helot), while being dressed up like wolves (werewolf motif) and by playing a 'dice' game with dog knuckles: (Greek kuon, Latin canicula).

In Vedic times they appear as vrātyas (*Atharvaveda* 15 and in many other passages); (Falk, 1986) they put pressure on their neighbours and gather cows as 'start capital'; they play a dice game (with 150 nuts) in the sabha outside the settlement by grabbing (glaha) an undefined number of nuts; the remnant must be divisible by 4 with exclaiming kṛta—'done!' The kali glaha with remnant 1 is the worst; the losing player is called śvaghnin 'characterized by dog killing.' Its equivalent in Indo–European archaeology was recently found at Krasnosamarskoye, just west of the Urals: this is a winter ritual of young men using small pieces of dog skulls (Anthony and Brown, 2017). Again archaeology, linguistics and texts overlap perfectly. Deities like the Gandharva (probably originally from the BMAC, Lubotsky, 2003) are prominent in the Hindu Kush area as wind/mountain spirits (the modern varoti < vātaputrī, Witzel, 2004) the 'fairies', the Apsaras-like Peri, likewise reside in the high mountain pastures. The ancient local god Indr appears even today as a horse-riding New Year visitor from the outside, etc., Newly adopted in this area are the Nāga, living in ice lakes and sending snow, as prominently found in the BMAC (Francfort, 1994), in Nuristan and Hindu Kush 'Peristan' and in Kashmir—all over the Dardic language area.

An even wider net has to be cast regarding some of these ancient myths and rituals: Indra's dragon slaying is closely reflected in Europe and even far away in Japanese myth and solemn ritual (Witzel, 2005). Many other myths and rituals, too, travelled well beyond Turan and India: the horse sacrifice (Puhvel, 1981) is found in the Veda, in ancient Rome, Ireland, in the steppe belt (including the Altai Turks as late as 1900 CE), in ancient Japan and in Northern China.

IN SUM

The complex Indian data exhibit many overlaps in archaeology, genetics, linguistics and Vedic texts. When comparing the results of these fields they largely agree with each other and sustain an emerging picture of the origin and spread of the Arya, their language, poetry, religion, ritual, culture, and even their genetic set-up.

The migration beyond the Upari Śyena mountains of the so-called Aryans, the self-designated Arya (Proto-Indo–Iranian), began in the southern Urals area, at the time of the invention of the light, horse-drawn chariot (2000 BCE) that was common to both pre-Iranian and pre-Vedic (Proto-Indo–Iranian *ratha,*rathaišta). It is attested in the Sintashta-Andronovo steppe cultures. This location is certain as Proto-Indo–Iranian (and Old Iranian later on) have transmitted a large amount of loanwords to the neighbouring forest dwellers, the speakers of the Proto–Uralic languages.

In the late second millennium the Proto-Indo–Iranians moved southwards, as is attested by their adoption of western Central Asian cultural features, ranging from agricultural terms of the BMAC to those of the religion and ritual of the Greater Bactrian area: deities like Indra, and the sacred drink Soma.

Part of this migration occurred via the Inner Asian Mountain corridor that had opened up for pastoral use after *c.*3000 BCE. It is here that the best Soma grows, where both the *Avesta* and the Veda locate the Muža/Mūja people and their spectacular Muzh mountain.

However, the Indo–Aryan language is first attested far away in the west, in the Mitanni realm of Northern Syria/ Iraq around 1400 BCE, with a single outlier of the marya-nnu charioteers already in 1761 BCE. The Indo–Aryans appearing in Mitanni probably moved via Bactria across Iran to the Zagros mountains, from where the Kassites too emerged, who then ruled Mesopotamia for half a millennium. Both these non-Indo–European languages have a substantial amount of early, pre-Vedic Indo–Aryan loanwords. Incidentally, these also furnish a date for the *Rig Veda*.

After passing through the BMAC and the adjacent mountain pastures of the Tian Shan/Pamirs, while retaining their language and most of their culture, the Indo–Aryans entered the valleys and high mountain pastures of the Hindu Kush, where they acquired some further traits of the local religion (Gandharva/Śarva; Apsaras, Nagas, the mineral kāca).

They then emerged on the western fringes of the Greater

Punjab around 1200 BCE, for example in Swat, where their aDNA has been discovered, along with the male steppe haplogroup R1a1 (some 30 per cent with the Kalasha, and still much found in modern North Indian Brahmins). This area was occupied by the Gandhara Grave Culture (1600 BCE) which initially, like the Kassites in Mesopotamia, may not have been Indo–Aryan speaking.

The contemporary situation in the Greater Punjab presented itself to the Indo–Aryans as a great opportunity, as the Harappan civilization had steadily been disintegrating. This was due to the general Near Eastern climate change, with increasing desiccation after 1900 BCE. Many if not most Indus inhabitants had moved to Haryana (or Gujarat). The wide open (uru-gavyūti, uloka) pastures of the Punjab allowed the semi-nomadic, largely pastoral Indo–Aryans an almost free range (*Aryavarta*) for their animals, mainly cattle and horses.

In the same area, the late Indus Civilization spanned the period from 1900-1300 BCE, which at the end perhaps marginally overlapped with the immigrating Indo–Aryans. The Indus populations were not homogenous as their isotopes and their aDNA (at Gonur and now apparently at Rakhigarhi) show. In fact, this was a multilingual area that delivered several substrates to Vedic Sanskrit, such as from Proto-Burushaski, the Para-Munda of the Punjab, and only late in the *Rig Veda*, from early Dravidian, which may have been spoken in adjoining Sindh.

As the Harappan culture was disintegrating into sparse village settlements, the Indo–Aryans could *no longer* acquire the prominent features of the mature Indus culture: the *Rig*

Veda does not show their international trade, seals, major deities, etc., However, there was communication with the remaining village population, as the approximately 300 loanwords in the hieratic *Rig Veda* text indicate. They deal with agriculture, music/dance, demons, etc.

That some of the elite of the remaining local Indus people was incorporated is indicated by the non-Indo–Aryan names of chieftains such as Balbutha, Bribu, and even that of the *Rig Veda* poets Kavasha and Kaṇva. This type of free admixture seems to end with the establishment of the four varnas (*Rig Veda* 10.90.12) that added the Shudra, while at the same time it excluded them from Arya religious practices—until today.

However, *mutual* influence between the two groups may be indicated by the change in burial practice from inhumation to cremation, as seen in the late Harappan urn with a homunculus bird motif (*c.*1300 BCE).

Just as the new genetic dates independently indicate the time of the migration, the actual composition of the *Rig Veda* too can be set at *c.*1200 BCE: it is a Late Bronze Age text that is linguistically younger than the Mitanni-Indo–Aryan (1400 BCE). The Iron Age first appears at locations such as Akra (west of the Indus) at *c.*1000 BCE. The poets of the *Rig Veda* continued to employ their inherited Indo–European/ Proto-Indo–Iranian-based language, their poetics, religion, ritual, the three-level class system, and some of the societal customs such as the sodality rituals of the vrātyas. However this ancient inheritance has been amalgamated with what the Indo–Aryans had picked up 'on the way': Soma, Indra, Gandharva, Nāgas, ṛṣi, atharvan, etc., by the time they moved into India across the Upari Śyena mountain.

In sum, neither was India ever isolated, nor did all facets of its archaeological, linguistic, textual, genetic/somatic data arise 'on their own' inside the Indian subcontinent; instead, they look back up to some 60,000 years of Out-of-Africa history. Just like other Asian subcontinents—Europe, the once dry Sundaland, Northeast Asia—the Indian subcontinent presents a fascinating array of internal developments and external influences that only patient and unbiased study can reveal.

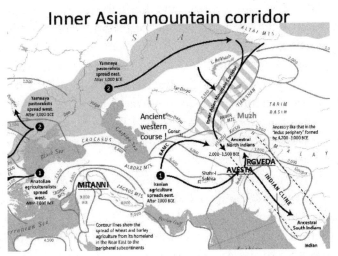

Spread of steppe pastoralists to Europe and to Western Central Asia and onwards to Swat in South Asia (3000–1250 BCE); courtesy V. Narasimhan, 2018

MULTIPLE THEORIES ABOUT THE 'ARYANS'

ROMILA THAPAR

I

THE BEGINNINGS

In any discussion of the 'Aryan' a good place to begin with would be to set out the space and time of the subject. In terms of space we tend to think only of the geography of the Indian subcontinent and the boundaries of pre-partition India as they existed for British India. The focus is then narrowed down to north-western India. But the geographical area of the archaeological and linguistic evidence is far more extensive. The links therefore are way beyond just the boundaries of north-west British India and involve some familiarity with more distant cultures.

In terms of archaeology, the more extensive earlier reach was that of the Harappa Culture or the Indus Civilization. From Shortughai in the Pamirs, evidence of Harappan settlements extends all the way south to the Indus plain and further to the Arabian Sea, westwards into Baluchistan and Makran and touching the Indo–Iranian borderlands, and eastwards into Punjab and Haryana. More recently finds have been located in Oman in the Arabian peninsula particularly in the vicinity of copper mines. The Harappans were known to have had trading relations with the Gulf and Mesopotamia. People of the ancient past did not confine themselves to one place. They travelled, migrated, traded and communicated across vast distances. This would probably have been too vast an area to host a single, unified culture. We have to consider the possibility of a multiplicity of cultures and societies, some fairly isolated and others in close contact but possibly functioning under a recognized and similar socio-political rubric.

Varieties of Indo–Aryan and Indo–Iranian speakers can only be given an approximate geographical location which is not as firm as that of archaeological cultures. The geographical area of all these languages is extensive but not all are referred to in the same text and they vary with the text. The wider geography of Proto-Indo–European takes a different direction from that of the Harappa Culture. Northern Syria and Anatolia are the locations possibly linked to Proto-Indo–Aryan, north-eastern Iran is the location for Old Iranian linked to the *Avesta,* and the speakers of Indo–Aryan as known from the *Rig Veda* are restricted to the Indo–Iranian borderlands and Punjab up to the Doab, which is geographically a small area. The history of the Indo–Aryan language has been extended backwards in time to the ancestral language of Indo–European and this brings in adjoining parts of Central Asia. The presence of Indo–Aryan in the Ganga plain is attested to in the post-Rigvedic period.

Thus although the focus is often only on the Punjab we should not forget that there was also a large area of West Asia and Central Asia that had a bearing on this history, even if the Indo–Aryan of the *Rig Veda* was not spoken in such a vast geographical area. The need for familiarity with the archaeology and linguistic history of other areas further complicates the problem. The geographical overlap between the Harappan sites and the place names associated with Indo–Aryan and Indo–Iranian is a limited area covering virtually only the Indo–Iranian borderlands and the Punjab. The thrust of the Harappan locations is southwards with maritime links westwards along the Persian Gulf, whereas the Indo–Aryan speakers show up overland and moving south-eastwards to the Ganga plain.

The chronology of the two is also different. The time bracket covers many centuries. There are some dates well established among historians and archaeologists. The Harappan urban cultures referred to as the Mature Harappan, date from about 2600 to about 1700 BCE, after urbanism slowly peters out. The *Rig Veda* is generally dated to the period after the decline of urbanism and would therefore date from about 1500 BCE or a couple of centuries later. The subsequent Vedas—the *Samaveda*, *Yajurveda* and *Atharvaveda*—relating also to the Ganga plain are dated to the early first millennium BCE.

However there are those who differ and would like to date the *Rig Veda* to 3000 BCE or even earlier and identify its culture with the Harappan cities. They maintain that the Aryans are indigenous and there was therefore not even a migration of any kind let alone any invasion as was thought in the nineteenth century. To maintain this position it is even said that the *Rig Veda* is prior to the Harappa Culture or that the authors of the Harappa Culture were Rigvedic Aryans. These views have become a matter of rather extensive controversy to say the least. This latter chronology, apart from not being able to muster firm evidence, creates huge problems for the historian. The discrepancy between Harappan urbanism and Rigvedic agro-pastoralism negates equivalence. Such an early chronology for the *Rig Veda* would, for example, create a gap of at least 1,500 years between the *Rig Veda* and the other Vedas and therefore break what is known to be the continuity between the four Vedas. Taking it back to the third millennium BCE creates major problems of parallels and correlations with archaeological evidence. It leads to a long chronological hiatus between the first and the later three Vedas—the *Samaveda, Yajurveda* and *Atharvaveda*—as the dating of these to the first millennium BC remains firm. Further, parts of the later Vedas are an exegesis on some Rigvedic hymns such that they indicate closeness in time between the earliest and the later Vedas. There is also a geographic shift from the upper Indus plain and its western borderlands which is substantially the location of the *Rig Veda*, to include the Ganga plain in the later three Vedas. The latter reflect societies in which the contours of varna as status groups, of economic occupations, of elements of kingship and rudimentary forms of authority have taken shape.

The insistence that the Aryans were a distinct people and that they were indigenous to the territory of British India is to impose present-day boundaries on the remote past which makes the statement anachronistic. Concepts such as 'indigenous' and 'alien' have to be precisely defined, which they are not in this case, and the definition has to conform to the time context for when it is being used. Those that we today call alien may not have been seen as such four thousand years ago. The same culture sometimes straddled across regions that in those times were seen as a unit but today is divided by national boundaries. Needless to say identities are never permanent or static throughout history.

If one seeks for a narrative of the beginnings of Indian history from Indian sources, such a narrative can be found in some of the Puranas. Written in the first millennium AD, these Puranas claim to refer to events of some millennia earlier. The earth was ruled by Manus and during the time of the seventh there was a great flood when everything was submerged. Manu, advised by Vishnu, had built a boat to carry him and the seven sages and others through the flood. Vishnu took the form of a fish, and Manu tied the boat to its horn. The fish swam through the waters and lodged the boat safely on a mountaintop. When the water subsided, Manu returned home. The progeny of Manu were ancestral to many lineages. Later kings seeking aristocratic status traced themselves back to these. Subsequent to these lineages there is a sequential listing of historically known dynasties. The intention therefore is to reflect a degree of historical perception and not restrict the narrative to a recitation of mythology. The myth has its own interest in terms of parallels with similar stories from ancient West Asia.[1]

---

[1]Romila Thapar, *Ancient Indian Social History: Some Interpretations*, Orient BlackSwan, 1978, pp. 264–65.

Significantly, this view of the beginnings of Indian history makes no mention of the original ancestors being 'Aryan', in part perhaps because 'Aryan' was not used invariably as an ethnic label. The names in the descent lists of the Puranas are not listed as Aryan or non-Aryan and the ancestry of some is distinctly uncertain. There was a traditional view therefore, in which 'the Aryan' as the initiator of history was absent. Arya was a status and used for a variety of respected persons. This changes however, in the nineteenth century narrative of the past where 'the Aryan' emerges as foundational to Indian history and the central figure of the narrative. This later version draws on a different body of texts, namely the Vedas, the earliest of which preceded these Puranas by about 1,500 years. The question then is that of what is being referred to by the term Arya in the Vedas, and subsequently in other texts, and how and why has the identity of 'the Aryan' been constructed and what changes has it undergone? This is not an academic question but central to how identities are constantly constructed and changed in every society throughout its history.

The Vedas were composed earlier than the Puranas, and were therefore in modern times taken as the starting point of Indian history. The earliest Veda was the *Rig Veda* and its hymns are dated to the latter part of the second millennium BCE. The Aryan identity was encouraged by the pre-eminence given to the Vedas by the Brahmanical tradition which also ensured that they became the primary texts for European scholars working on Indian civilization. But there was also a more evident European context that gave form to the theory about the Aryans as it developed in the nineteenth century.

Officers of the East India Company serving in India began to explore the history and culture of the colony they were governing. This was both out of curiosity about governing a singularly alien culture and out of a conviction that an effective control over society required knowledge of its history, and if the knowledge was not readily available it would have to be discovered. The time was the late eighteenth century when new ideas of the Enlightenment were in the air. Knowledge about the Indian past, referred to as 'the furniture of empire' was viewed as providing an access to power. Governing a colony required familiarity with the local languages, laws and religions since these were seen as the constituents of its culture. History was defined in accordance with Enlightenment definitions and such histories were not available in the corpus of Sanskrit literature, regarded as the pre-eminent intellectual corpus of the Indian pre-colonial period. The history of early India therefore as now constructed would have an emphasis on tested chronology and sequential narrative.

Early explorations were dominated by the need to construct a chronology for the Indian past. Attempts were made to trace parallels with Biblical narratives and chronology. But the exploration with the maximum potential lay in the study of languages and particularly Sanskrit. Interest in these studies was enhanced with the recognition that there were similarities between Sanskrit and the classical languages of Europe.[2] This had been referred to in previous centuries by merchants and missionaries visiting India. The most widely quoted among these was an Italian merchant Filippo Sassetti who in the sixteenth century suggested a link between Sanskrit and some European languages. These comments gave way to more systematic studies by Sir William Jones and his colleagues working in various administrative positions of the East India Company, who began researching into Sanskrit and local languages such as Bengali, Urdu and Hindi in the late eighteenth and early nineteenth century.

William Jones was intrigued by what he saw as parallels between Greco–Roman deities and those of the Hindu pantheon as also by the possibility of comparing Biblical and Hindu mythological narratives to provide chronological clues. But his more lasting work was in the comparative study of languages. William Jones wrote not only on the excellent qualities of Sanskrit as a language but also argued that it was a cognate of Greek, Latin and Persian, and that all of them doubtless had a common ancestor. The notion of monogenesis—the single origin of all these languages— was extended to the speakers of the languages as well. This slippage between speech and biology was to dominate the nineteenth centuries.

At Chennai, somewhat later, the work of Ellis and still later Caldwell is associated with analytical studies of Telugu

---

[2]William Jones, 'Third Anniversary Discourse', *Asiatic Researches*, 1788, pp. 415–31.

and Tamil.[3] The difference between what came to be known as the Indo–Aryan languages and the Dravidian languages was noted by both the British scholars and by the pandits— who were providing information on Sanskrit and Telugu. What this pointed to was that Sanskrit was not ancestral to all the Indian languages and that the Dravidian group had other roots. Prior to the spread of Indo–Aryan, the Dravidian languages were used in various parts of the subcontinent as is also evident from linguistic remnants to this day. A possible borrowing between the various groups of languages would be expected where they were contiguous. The recognition that there were other languages contemporary with Indo–Aryan such as those of the Dravidian and Austro–Asiatic families required the examining of their relationships.

The possibility of comparing languages encouraged the evolution of philology in European universities and it became the forerunner to modern linguistics—the science of language. The Vedic corpus became available in the early nineteenth century to scholars in Europe and furthered the interest in comparative philology. These studies gradually envisaged an Indo–European family of languages descended from an ancestral language. The idea that the identity of speech and of people coincided meant that by the latter half of the nineteenth century European scholarship searched for

---

[3]R. Caldwell, *A Comparative Grammar of the Dravidian or South Indian Family of Languages*, London: Trubner & Co, Ludgate Hill, 1856; P. W. Ellis, 1816, 'Note to the Introduction', included in A. D. Campbell, *A Grammar of the Teloogoo Language*, quoted in part in T. Trautmann, ed., *The Aryan Debate*, New Delhi: Oxford University Press, 2005.

the homeland of a people, the Indo–Europeans, a search in part encouraged by German Romanticism.[4]

This was given a further impetus by the prevailing theory of discrete civilizations. The world was divided into self-sufficient civilizations demarcated by language and religion. India, therefore, was the civilization of the Sanskrit language and the Hindu religion. Sanskrit was said to be the oldest surviving Indo–European language, although the proto-language had to be reconstructed through back formation from the later languages. However, this was an easy step to seeing Sanskrit as the ancestral language as some did and still do. German Romanticism was partial to this idea. Herder and Schlegel suggested that the roots of human history might go back to the beginnings recorded in Sanskrit texts.

Comparative philologists such as E. Burnouf and F. Bopp were primarily interested in the technicalities of analysing language. Philological studies delved into the grammatical structure of Panini's treatment of classical Sanskrit and this was in some ways new to European linguistic studies. Indo–European, reconstructed from the daughter languages, was traced back to a Central Asian homeland. Europe was on the edge of an Oriental Renaissance. It was believed that yet another Renaissance might follow from the discovery of the Orient and this would take knowledge into yet other directions.[5]

---

[4]A. Leslie Willson, *A Mythical Image: The Ideal of India in German Romanticism*, Durham: Duke University Press, 1964; J. Drew, *India and the Romantic Imagination*, New Delhi: Oxford University Press, 1987.

[5]R. Schwab, (trans.) Gene Patterson-Black and Victor Reinking, *The*

Those who spoke languages derived from Indo–European, came to be referred to by various labels, but ultimately 'Aryan' became the accepted one by the middle of the nineteenth century. Taken from references in the *Rig Veda* where the authors of the hymns refer to themselves as Arya, and from the Iranian *Avesta* where the term is Airiia, in neither case however, was it used in a racial sense. For philologists, Aryan indicated a language and therefore meant, 'an Aryan-speaking person'. This was frequently abbreviated to Aryan and came to be applied incorrectly as a racial label.

II
ASSOCIATION WITH RACE

This interest in the 'Aryan' coincided with the theories of the French diplomat, Joseph Arthur Comte de Gobineau who was searching for Aryan identities in Europe and warning against interbreeding between what was beginning to be described as Aryan and non-Aryan people.[6] Classification according to race was borrowed from biological studies such as the principles of Linnaeus for defining genera and species, as also the theory of the survival of the fittest, and both were applied to human societies. Races were arranged in a hierarchy from advanced to backward. What has been described as 'race-science' was viewed as an accurate identification of human

---

Oriental Renaissance: Europe's Rediscovery of India and the East, 1680-1880, New York: Columbia University Press, 1984.

[6]Léon Poliakov, *The Aryan Myth: A History of Racist and Nationalist Ideas in Europe*, (Trans.) Edmund Howard, New York: Basic Books, 1974.

groups.[7] Race shifted the focus of Europe's origins from possible Biblical beginnings to what was thought of as the more 'scientific' understanding of origins in the form of races.

In many ways race was invented by European colonialism. The demonstrated success of imperialism and the view that European nations were the most advanced, in contrast to the colonized who were thought of as the lesser breeds, reinforced these identities, as also did some aspects of Social Darwinism. These ideas acted as a factor in changing the European view of its origins.

The intersection of Europe and Asia, and the resulting philological studies, particularly in German and French thought, had earlier played with ideas of possible Oriental origins. German Romanticism in the earlier part of the nineteenth century portrayed Sanskrit and Indian culture as encapsulating the noble beginnings of universal civilization. Sanskrit was described as the parent language and the Aryans of India as the font of civilization and from whom there was a dispersal of culture and language to other parts of the world. From various perspectives Asia became the focus of historical investigation.

Parallel to this was another line of thinking current in Germany. This was influenced by a search for origins and identities in the later nineteenth century not unconnected with ideas of nationalism. It had been argued that the Roman empire declined from the fifth century CE because of frequent

---

[7]Nancy Stepan, *The Idea of Race in Science: Great Britain 1800-1960*, London: Palgrave Macmillan, 1982.

attacks by the German and other tribes on northern Europe who were regarded as barbarians by the Romans. These attributes of the tribes gradually changed from their being barbaric to their being heroic and invincible, creating and defending the kingdoms they established in medieval times in northern Europe. A consciousness of pan-Germanism gradually took root. More importantly, Tacitus, a Roman historian of the first century CE who had written about the purity of blood of the German tribes was frequently quoted.[8] Purity of blood became the criterion of racial superiority. The German tribes were said to constitute the original people, the Urvolk, and their language was the original language, the Ursprache. This demarcated them from other communities in Europe where both language and race had been contaminated.

Such ideas were common currency in much of Europe with various communities claiming the status of superior Aryans. Imperial powers experienced a certain hesitation if not embarrassment at admitting to a common origin with some of the communities of Asia. Given this, it was inevitable that the original Aryan people would have to be geographically relocated in some part of Europe. The Aryans were divided into Asian and European. The former had their homeland in Central Asia and the latter were said to have originated from the Nordic blondes of northern Europe.[9] This

---

[8]Publius Cornelius Tacitus, *Germania*, pp. 2, 4.
[9]Isaac Taylor, *The Origin of the Aryans: An Account of the Prehistoric Ethnology and Civilisation of Europe*, London: Walter Scott Ltd, 1889.

was facilitated by the claim that the descendants of Indo–Europeans had diverse skull types as revealed by craniology. The measurement of the cephalic index and the nasal index as indicators of race was to be enthusiastically adopted in India, as for example by Herbert Risley.[10]

The equation of language with race was made with increasing frequency. Its presence has also been noticed in the initial reconstruction of the history and civilization of the ancient Greeks. Less credence was given to possible Mesopotamian and Egyptian antecedents with a preference for treating ancient Greek culture as an Aryan creation, introduced through the conquest of Greece by an Aryan people. From this point on the Aryan became axiomatic to the study of human typology. It was to have disastrous consequences in twentieth century Germany with the Nazi ideology proclaiming the superiority of the Aryan race.

The theory of Aryan race also came to be viewed as foundational to Indian history largely through what has been called the twinning of the theories of British Sanskritists and ethnographers.[11] Max Müller's influential role lay in his projecting Indian civilization primarily through the prism of what he constructed as the culture of the Vedas. He edited the *Rig Veda* together with the fourteenth century commentary on the text by Sayana. For Max Müller the *Rig Veda* was the earliest stratum of Indo–European and therefore the most

---

[10]H. H. Risley, *The People of India*, London: W. Thacker & Co, 1908.
[11]T. R. Trautmann, *Aryans and British India*, New Delhi: Oxford University Press, 1997.

ancient literature in the world and the key to the earliest language and religion of India. He maintained that there was an original Aryan homeland in Central Asia from where there was a dispersal of Aryan speakers branching off in two directions.[12]One went to Europe and the other migrated to Iran eventually splitting again with one segment invading north-western India. The references in the *Rig Veda* to the Aryas and to their hostility towards the Dasas were read as the Aryans invading and enslaving the indigenes—the Dasas, and eventually settling in India. The reference to Arya-varna and Dasa-varna/the Arya and Dasa colour, was understood to mean skin pigmentation and seen as a description of fair-skinned Aryans conquering the dark-skinned aborigines. Despite his including the commentary of Sayana, Max Müller paid little attention to the explanations in the commentary. However fanciful at times there was no reference to race.

The northern Aryans migrated to Europe, the southern Aryans migrated to Iran and to India. The Aryas developed Vedic Sanskrit as their ritual language. They were segregated from the Dasas through the instituting of caste. The upper-caste Hindus were taken as biological, lineal descendants of the Aryans. The lower castes, untouchables and tribals were descended from the Dasas. As was common in the nineteenth century Max Müller used a number of words interchangeably, such as Hindu/Indian/race/nation/people/blood, words

---

[12]Max Müller, *Lectures on the Science of Language*, London: Longmans, Green & Co, 1862; *India: What Can it Teach Us?* London: Longmans, Green & Co, 1883; *Biographies of Words and the Home of the Aryas*, London: Longmans, Green & Co, 1888.

whose meanings would today be carefully differentiated.

Although in the ancient texts Aryan was specifically a label for a language and a social status, in the nineteenth century it came to be used indiscriminately for a race as well, both in Europe and in India. Max Müller denied any link between language and race, when he stated that, 'Aryan in scientific language is utterly inapplicable to race. It means language and nothing but language...'[13] But there was often confusion between language and race. It was thought that those who spoke the same language were inevitably members of the same biological race. History has proved this to be entirely erroneous. The same language can be spoken by members of more than one race or one ethnic group depending on the historical need for the language. Even Max Müller was given to confusing the two. The sliding from language to race became frequent in contemporary thinking. An equally erroneous equation in South Asia was that of the Dravidian languages with a Dravidian race. The structure of Indo–Aryan and Dravidian languages differed hence it was maintained that they represented a racial differentiation as well. Furthermore, it was held that since Indo–Aryan came from outside, the speakers of Dravidian were native to India.

The reconstruction of what was believed to be Aryan history superseded the initial eighteenth century Orientalist search for Biblical connections and parallels even in the early

---

[13]Max Müller, *Auld Lang Syne*, New York: Charles Scribner's Sons, 1898, p. 90.

history of India. There was now briefly, a focus on common Aryan origins with Europe. This included a dismissal of the intervention of the Semitic peoples and languages, both in European and Indian culture. There was such an emphatic focus on the Vedas that even the Puranas were for Max Müller second order knowledge. As we have seen, the Puranic version of historical genesis did not involve Aryas and Dasas or any ethnic groups. The exclusion of the Semitic meant an exclusion of any Islamic contribution to Indian civilization in the perspective of Max Müller. As with many British scholars he refers to the tyranny of Mohammedan rule in India but does not explain why he thought it was tyrannical. The Hindus were frequently viewed as the indigenous people who were conquered and then oppressed by the Muslims. Further, that the coming of British rule meant that the Hindus were rid of oppressive Muslim rule now replaced by benevolent British rule.[14]

The equation of language and race was instrumental in the formulating of the theory. Aryan conquest was seen as introducing both the Indo–Aryan language brought by people of the Aryan race and also what has come to be described as the distinctive Aryan civilization. This became the opening narrative of Indian history. It was acceptable to historians who at the time often ascribed the explanation of events to conquest. The theory was attractive to colonial thinking because it provided an antecedent to the British conquest

---

[14]H. M. Elliot and J. Dowson, *The History of India as Told by its Own Historians*, London: Trubner & Co., 1869, p. xxii.

of India and the introduction of what was believed to be an imported civilization through this process, a view which is partially responsible for the current rejection in some circles of the Aryans being other than indigenous.

It also allowed for another explanation. Racial separateness required a demarcating feature and conquest became the mechanism by which caste hierarchy and inequalities could be explained as a form of racial segregation. Since caste was central to Indian social institutions, racial segregation by this logic played the same role. Caste became more comprehensible if it was explained merely as racial segregation rather than by the more complex theories involving kinship, occupations, and rules of purity and pollution. Indian history was gradually being brought into the current European discourse on race.

The idea of the separation of the European from the Asian Aryans entered the discussion when colonial policy drew a sharp distinction between the colonizer and the colonized. The equality of European and Asian Aryans began slowly to be denied. Such a denial was necessary for those who proposed a radical social and economic restructuring of the colony through legislation and administration so that the colony would be converted into a viable source of revenue. Discussion on such matters was current among Utilitarian thinkers, the Free Trade lobby and economists such as Adam Smith. At the same time those who supported Orientalist views on the Indian past were sympathetic to the theory since it gave pre-eminence to the Brahmanas and to their authorship of the Vedas.

Caste as racial segregation, separating the upper caste Aryan from the lower caste non-Aryan, was viewed as a scientific way of organizing society in keeping with modern ideas. When the rigidity of caste was criticized, especially by missionaries, it was accepted that this weakened Indian society, particularly in its confrontation with Islam. Caste was divisive and therefore a united front against invaders was not possible—an argument that is still heard from people who forget that substantial campaigns within India between Hindu rulers were equally destructive of the social fabric. It was also said that caste saved Hinduism from being absorbed into other religions and helped maintain its identity. That conversion to the other religions often carried the caste identity with it was not recognized. Nor did the status of the untouchable change on conversion. There were few analyses where caste was seen to have its own history of adaptation and change. Moralizing on the evils of caste precluded the need to see it as an agency of power, dominance and subordination, or to recognize the large area of negotiation which permitted some castes to shape their status.

The theory was popularized in India through the views of Max Müller. It was also taken up by those working on the early Sanskrit texts such as John Muir (1874) and John Wilson (1877). The latter, as missionaries, were critical of the inequities of caste and drew attention to the plight of the lower castes. They now argued that the lower castes who were the indigenous inhabitants were oppressed by the Brahmanas who were the Aryas and came as invaders. There was a conflict between the Aryas and the non-Aryas, and the

term Arya also came to be used as a patronymic referring
to the Aryan people.

III

JYOTIBA PHULE AND B. G. TILAK

Such views were becoming familiar to many Indians. Among
them, a radical turn was provided by Jyotiba Phule whose
perceptions were very different from the concerns of
European comparative philologists and supporters of race
science. Writing in the latter half of the nineteenth century
in Marathi, Phule argued that the original inhabitants of India
were the Adivasis, among whom he included the Shudras,
Ati Shudras and Dalits, all of whom were descendants of
the heroic peoples led by the Daitya king, Bali.[15] Various
such categories were included under the generic title of
Kshatriya. The Adivasis fought the arrival of the Brahmanas
who represented the Aryans, but were conquered and
subordinated. Phule draws on well-known myths to
emphasize his point.

Phule's version has become essential to the Dalit
perspective on Indian history. It was also to influence a
number of the non-Brahmin movements in the peninsula.
The dichotomy between Brahmin and non-Brahmin slid
easily into the linguistic division of Aryan and Dravidian
languages where the former language was said to be of the
former group and the latter language of the latter groups. The

---

[15]G. P. Deshpande, ed., *Selected Writings of Jotirao Phule*, Delhi: Manohar,
2002.

language demarcation was an important component of the social divide.[16] The rejection of Aryan dominance implied a rejection of the Indo–Aryan languages. Phule's interpretation of the theory made caste the differentiating feature rather than race or religion in explaining the beginnings of history. In this interpretation the lower castes had a chronological priority in their identity with the land.

The upper castes had their own use for the theory of the Aryan race and it was again given a turn that suited their social aspirations and political needs. The views of Phule were generally ignored. B. G. Tilak, also from Maharashtra but writing in English, endorsed the antiquity of the *Rig Veda* by taking it back to 4500 BC, considerably earlier than the date of 1500 BCE given by Max Müller. Tilak based his argument on his readings of what he claimed were planetary positions referred to in the hymns.[17] Accepting the theory of the Nordic homeland for European Aryans, Tilak maintained that the Aryans had trekked from the Arctic in the post-glacial age and then branched off, one group settling in Europe and the other travelling to the Indian subcontinent. The European Aryans relapsed into barbarism, but those that settled in India retained their original superior culture which they imposed on the local non-Aryans. Sometime later when objections were raised to Tilak having supported the theory

---

[16]S. Ramaswamy, *Passions of the Tongue*, Berkeley: University of California Press, 1997.

[17]B. G. Tilak, *Orion or Researches into the Antiquity of the Vedas*, Bombay: Mrs Radhabai Atmaram Sagoon, 1893; *The Arctic Home in the Vedas*, Poona: Messrs, Tilak Bros, 1903.

that the Aryans came from outside India, the objections were set aside by some people arguing that in those early times the North Pole was within the territory of British India![18] Max Müller was familiar with Tilak's ideas although not in agreement with them, but he did incidentally help in getting Tilak released from jail when he was incarcerated by the British for nationalist activities.

The theory was used by some to argue for the superiority of the upper castes and to promote their self-esteem by maintaining that not only were the upper castes the lineal descendants of the Aryans but that they were also racially related to the European Aryan. Keshab Chunder Sen follows Max Müller and John Wilson when he states that, '...in the advent of the English nation in India we see a reunion of parted cousins, the descendants of two different families of the ancient Aryan race.'[19] The theory of common origins strengthened a possible link between the colonizers and the Indian upper caste elite. The superiority of the Aryan was an inheritance from nineteenth century theories and is one of the factors in the current insistence largely by non-historians that the Aryan should be indigenous to India.

Views such as these coincided with the emergence of nationalism in the late nineteenth century articulated mainly by the middle class, drawn from the upper castes. In a period of rapid social change even these groups were seeking both

---

[18]A. C. Das, *Rigvedic India*, Calcutta: University of Calcutta, 1920.

[19]K. C. Sen, *Keshub Chunder Sen's Lectures in India*, London: Cassell and Company, Limited, 1904.

legitimacy and identity from the past. Origins therefore became crucial. Aryan origins and lineal descent were emphasized and appropriated by the upper castes. Other castes and non-Hindus were either marginalized or excluded. Aryanism therefore became an exclusive status conditioned by birth. Biological status was coming back through a circuitous way and the qualification of language was receding. Nevertheless Aryan and non-Aryan differentiation which had been of an ethnic and racial kind was also beginning to touch implicitly on class differentiation.

Nationalisms of various kinds—anti-colonial, religious, regional, linguistic—demand theories of origins and identities, perhaps more insistently than other political movements. These theories resort to their versions of history and particularly the beginnings of history, drawing attention to when a society believes it was founded. Therefore, Aryanism having become foundational to Indian history, new nationalisms reinterpreted the theories to support their political aspirations.

The reverse but parallel image as it were of Phule's thesis was that expounded by Dayanand Saraswati, a Brahmana learned in the Shastras and who has also been described as a social reformer. He founded the Arya Samaj, an organization seeking to return to what it interpreted as the social and religious life of the Vedas. These texts became the blueprint of Dayanand's vision of Indian society as set out in his best-known work, *Satyartha Prakash*. He argued that the Vedas are the source of all knowledge including modern science. He underlined the linguistic and racial purity of the Aryans. The Arya Samaj was seen by its followers as 'the society of the Aryas'. The upper castes were the Aryas. Dalits were excluded, but through the innovation of a ritual called shuddhi or purification, it was possible for some lower castes to claim higher status. The notion of their having to go through 'purification' is an indication of upper caste contempt. Dayanand stated that the Aryans, the authors of the Vedas, migrated into India from Tibet, although there was no evidence to suggest this connection with Tibet.

Dayanand had parleyed with another group that had firm ideas about the Aryans and the beginnings of Indian history. For a brief while the Theosophical Society and the Arya Samaj were virtually merged, but soon they fell apart. Neither Madame Blavatsky and Colonel Olcott who founded the Theosophical Society in 1875, nor Dayanand were exactly people who easily accommodated themselves to divergent views. Madame Blavatsky spent much of her time establishing centres in different parts of the world in order to legitimize her version of the occult. She fostered, however briefly, an interest in current nationalisms such as in Ireland and India. But her more lasting imprint was on centres in Europe that nurtured Ariosophist thinking involved with notions of Aryan superiority. Such centres were often the crucible of Aryan racism.[20] In India the more active person was Colonel Olcott. He regarded the Aryans as the ancestors of modern Hindus, and as indigenous to India, and that these same

---

[20]N. Goodrick Clarke, *The Occult Roots of Nazism*, New York: I. B. Tauris, 1992.

Aryans had been the progenitors of European civilization.[21] This was an echo of some of the earlier ideas of German Romanticism in relation to India.

These varied versions of the theory and the issues that they were concerned with did not die out at the end of the nineteenth century but have lived vicariously through some of the social movements and political ideologies of the twentieth century. For example, the current notion being propagated that Hindus are descended from indigenous Aryans, was earlier expressed in the Theosophical reading of the Aryan theory as argued by Colonel Olcott. The Theosophical theory that the Aryans took civilization from India to the West is being repeated. That Indian communities lived in harmony with each other and contentions came only with the arrival of 'the Muslims' comes from colonial views.

Some of those writing at the popular level in the early twentieth century, who were connected to what became the Rashtriya Swayamsevak Sangh (RSS), the central organization of the Hindu Right, redefined the Indian and the Aryan identity, to give priority to a religious identity. Caste Hindus were Aryans and Aryans were indigenous to India. Non-Hindus were foreign and these were the Muslims, Christians, Parsis, and the Communists as well. All these were aliens since India was neither the land of their birth

---

[21]J. Leopold, 'British Applications of the Aryan Theory of Race to India, 1850–70', *The English Historical Review*, 89, 1975, pp. 578–603; 'The Aryan Theory of Race in India 1870–1920, Nationalist and Internationalist Visions', *Indian Economic and Social History Review*, 1970, VII, 2, pp. 271–98.

and ancestry—Pitribhumi—nor the place where their religion originated—Punyabhumi.[22] There had been at one point a collapsing of the racial identity with nationalism and at another a shift from race to caste. The use of the word jati for both caste and race added to the confusion. Although jati is linked to birth it also draws on a variety of social and religious activities which continually change the parameters of caste identity. The racial identity is so deeply ingrained in the concept of the Aryan that references to 'the Aryan race' are common in the media and in the conversation of large numbers of people in India. However, when the identity shifted to a more clearly religious one as in the equation of Aryan with Hindu, as it has now done, then the meaning of Aryan also changed, although the fuzziness often continues.

This range of interpretations of the Aryan theory illustrates how it came to be used in the agendas of various social and political groups and their contestations. It reflects an imagined ethnicity being presented as an explanation for the organization of a society. The explanation takes on the coloration of scientific approval where biological heredity is made to coincide with categories of language. The history of a nation is sought to be traced with authority vesting in contemporary upper castes or those of the dominant religion. Alternatively, a demand is made for the restitution of rights of those who see themselves as having been denied their claim

---

[22]V. D. Savarkar, *Hindutva: Who is a Hindu?*, Bombay: Veer Savarkar Prakashan, 1922; M. S. Golwalkar, *We, Or Our Nationhood Defined*, Nagpur: Bharat Publications, 1938.

to being the true inheritors of the land. Identities of race, caste and religion underline separateness. They also attempt to provide seemingly easy explanations of social insecurities, however invalid these may be as historical explanations.

IV

THE INDUS CIVILIZATION

These varied versions of the theory and the forms they took in the nineteenth and early twentieth century faced another set of problems with the archaeological discovery of the Indus Civilization from 1922–23 onwards. The excavation of the cities of Harappa and Mohenjodaro and subsequent excavations in India and Pakistan revealing an extensive urban culture distributed across the Indus plain and into Gujarat and Haryana, created problems for the earlier simpler versions of the Aryan theory. The cities were found to date to the early third millennium and therefore represented the culture that initiated Indian civilization. Being predominantly urban, the Indus Civilization is viewed by scholars as distinctively different from the agro-pastoralists familiar from the Vedas and particularly the earliest *Rig Veda*. The Vedas are primarily ritual texts so their representation of society is somewhat indirect. The archaeological evidence, and particularly data relating to environment, technology and economy, covers a wider area and goes further back in time, and because it is most commonly in the form of an artefact it has precision. It has therefore come to be seen as the primary data for the reconstruction of the earliest history of India. This creates a problem for those who would still like to see the Vedic corpus as the earliest evidence of Indian history. Because these texts were used in reconstructing history prior to the discovery of the archaeological evidence, there is a tendency for the archaeological data to be read in the light of the Vedic corpus.

The idea of identifying the Indus cities with the authors of Vedic culture was initially put forward by L. A. Waddell in 1925, working on Sumerian links but bringing in current readings of the role of the Aryan.[23] Other archaeologists maintained that the cities were built by pre-Aryans and subsequently destroyed by the Aryans. The discovery of the Indus cities was also used, to the contrary, as grist to the mill of Dravidian nationalism claiming that the Harappans were Dravidian-speaking and that the civilizational roots of India were therefore Dravidian.[24] A Dravidian identity remains an undercurrent in the identification of the Indus Civilization. The claim tends to be rather brushed aside by the much more vocal insistence on Indo–Aryan roots through identifying the authors of the Harappan Culture with the Aryans who composed the *Rig Veda*. These claims and counterclaims will continue until the pictograms/script remains undeciphered.

In pursuing the various ways in which the Aryan theory was used it is often forgotten that professional Indian historians distance themselves from popular theories. Popular discussions of Indian views of the Aryans seldom quote historians but frequently quote Aurobindo, Vivekananda,

---

[23]L. A. Waddell, *The Indo-Sumerian Seals Deciphered*, London: Luzac & Co., 1925.
[24]S. Ramaswamy, *Passions of the Tongue*, Berkeley: University of California Press, 1997.

Dayanand and Tilak, who were primarily men of learning, with strong political agendas. They are sometimes described as representing the age-old Hindu intellectual tradition, a statement that overlooks the fact that they were essentially arguing within a colonial dialogue. The claim that the focus was on roots and traditions did not however draw on Sayana and his predecessors but was in the context of various contemporary nationalisms including a reaction to colonial interpretations of the Indian past. The mix of anti-colonialism and religious revivalism varied in these nationalisms. Historians were not claiming to represent a tradition. The classic history by Hemchandra Raychaudhuri first published in 1923, *Political History of Ancient India*, begins with the accession of Parikshit, subsequent to the war in the Mahabharata, and there is an association with the supposed start of the Kali Yuga after the war. Almost throughout the twentieth century historians kept a close track on the evidence being revealed by excavations apart from the reading of the texts. However, what was left unaddressed was the more fundamental question of the perspective implicit in the colonial construction of the Aryan identity and the implications of this construction for Indian history.

After the discovery of the Indus cities most histories began by describing them as the starting point of Indian civilization and then proceeded to speak of a Vedic age as the successor. The rise of the cities were dated to the third millennium BCE and the *Rig Veda* to anywhere between 1500 and 1200 BCE. The cultural identity of the Indus cities remained uncertain, but the coming of 'the Aryans' was attributed to an invasion. Max Müller's theory of an invasion was reiterated by Mortimer Wheeler in his work on the archaeology of the cities. But gradually, the interweaving of archaeological and linguistic data—to the extent that this was possible—began to question such an invasion. With historical analysis increasingly approximating the methods of the social sciences, invasion as the invariable explanation of historical change was being questioned. The linguistic evidence in particular pointed towards multiple small migrations and other changes in the cultural landscape of those times.[25]

In Europe scholars began to move away from pursuing origins and identities and broadened the parameters of Indo–European studies to include many more societies using languages associated with Indo–European. Although the study of comparative philology continued there was an added interest in comparative mythology. The exclusiveness of a single language group began to be questioned by the suggestion that there was a recognizable structural similarity and shared ideology across a spectrum of societies using languages of the Indo–European family. This, according to Georges Dumézil, was expressed in a common pattern of social organization which he called the Three Orders—priests, a warrior aristocracy and the pastoralists and cultivators—which was present in the mythology of these groups. Myths

---

[25]Romila Thapar, 'Society in Ancient India: The Formative Period', 1969, reprinted in R. Thapar, *Cultural Pasts: Essays in Early Indian History*, New Delhi: Oxford University Press, 2000, pp. 310–35; 'Archaeology and Language at the Roots of Ancient India', *Journal of the Asiatic Society of Bombay*, 64–66 (n.s.), 1989–91, pp. 249–68.

reflected the function of each group.[26] Although it was demonstrated that the theory of the Three Orders could be applied to non-Indo–European-language-using societies as well, and therefore did not have a specificity relating to particular language groups, it did, nevertheless, shift the sights of research to new perspectives. The archaeological hunt for the Aryans became less insistent. But the search for the Indo–European homeland continued. Marija Gimbutas suggested that the Kurgan graves of Central Asia were associated with the Indo–European speakers.[27] Colin Renfrew argued for the diffusion of farming communities from Anatolia in preference to horse-riding and chariot-using elites spreading from Central Asia.[28] Neither of these hypotheses has, however, provided the answer but the geography of the study went beyond India.

In India, the attempt to correlate archaeological and textual data took other forms. From the middle of the century when information from excavations was increasing, it began to be juxtaposed to the textual information of the earliest texts. Initially there was a bifurcation between histories based on the two categories of sources but attempts began to be made to integrate the evidence, which, of course, was difficult

---

[26]C. Scott Littleton, *The New Comparative Mythology: An Anthropological Assessment of the Theories of Georges Dumézil*, Berkeley: University of California Press, 1973.

[27]M. Gimbutas, *The Kurgan Culture and the Indo-Europeanization of Europe*, Washington DC: Institute for the Study of Man, 1997.

[28]C. Renfrew, *Archaeology and Language: The Puzzle of Indo-European Origins*, Cambridge: Cambridge University Press, 1987.

in most cases. The reading of archaeological evidence, as indeed of linguistic evidence as well, has its own rules. This is something that is not always remembered. Furthermore, if the evidence from archaeology differs from that which comes from textual sources the attempt should not be to force a fit between the two but rather to try and understand what the evidence from each may be saying. This also requires that in commenting on these sources we need to be familiar with recent discoveries and interpretations and the rigour of the discipline in question.

The need, therefore, is to understand the parameters of the Harappan cities and not just to relate stray items of material culture to objects described in textual sources. There are a number of problems that have to be contended with in suggesting a correlation. As I have said earlier, the geographical boundaries of the city civilization extend far beyond those of the geography known to the *Rig Veda*, with connections to the Gulf and Mesopotamia. The Indus cities as urban centres were dependent on a substantial agrarian production and agro-pastoral production alone would not have sufficed. This is attested by plough agriculture and granaries. A gradual change from village settlement to urban centre can be observed in association with the cities, as for example, in the vicinity of Mehrgarh in Baluchistan. Urban structures of importance are sometimes built on extensive brick platforms; the city plan is carefully worked out including a remarkable system of drainage; there are impressive fortifications; and the residential area has large familial houses with civic amenities. Centres of craft production were linked to local and long distance trade. All this required arrangements for obtaining and controlling labour, gathering raw material, organizing production and networks of exchange. The symbols on the seals and elsewhere have been taken as indications of a script, or a system of communication used presumably for identifying persons and products. Clearly, urbanization as a pattern of living was a familiar experience to the Harappans.

Such parameters are not recognizable in the *Rig Veda*. This text is a collection of hymns yet even the religious articulation of these find little correlation with artefacts from the cities.[29] However significant and evocative the hymns of the *Rig Veda* may be, and many are associated with a recognizable awareness of religious belief and ritual, the societies that can be visualized through them are of relatively small groups of agro-pastoralists, living in villages, herding cattle and tending fields. Their wealth is computed primarily in horses and cows hence the importance of the cattle-raid as an activity and the frequency of skirmishes probably over pastures and water sources. The horse had enormous functional importance as well as a ritual presence. Movements of people can occasionally be inferred and the general direction was from the north-west towards the Indo–Gangetic watershed[30], later moving into the Ganga plain.

The discussion on the chronological priority and the identity of the Indus Civilization and the Vedic corpus

[29]'The Archaeological Background to the Agnicayana Ritual', in F. Staal et al. (eds.), *Agni*, Berkeley: University of California Press, 1983, pp. 1–40.
[30]Thapar, *Cultural Pasts*, 2000, pp. 310–335.

entered standard histories from the middle of the last century.[31] But by the last decade of the century some of the discussion began to incorporate political intentions. If now it is to avoid becoming self-defeating, it is necessary that it remain a scholarly debate and that historical methodology be observed. Ascertaining Aryan identities are of interest to 'the Aryan linguistic diaspora' in Eurasia. In India, however, the subject is now enmeshed in cultural politics. The theory of the indigenous origin of Aryans is necessary to the ideology of Hindu nationalism and it seeks to set aside scholarly analysis in the claims being made. Others argue that in a post-colonial context, theories emerging from such 'nationalisms' must receive serious attention not as scholarship, but as aspects of nationalism. Further, that excluding them from discussion is contributing to a sort of Indological McCarthyism where the challenging of long-held assumptions pertaining to the Indo–Aryans are dubbed fundamentalist, nationalist and contributing to Nazi agendas.[32] Are we then to concede to the academic fashions that maintain that all theories of explanation have equal validity and should receive equal attention; or that earlier theories having arisen in a colonial context, contemporary theories coming from 'nationalist' concerns have to be given the benefit of the doubt, even if such theories are borrowing from colonial interpretations that now have little scholarly validity? Such concessions are

---

[31]R. C. Majumdar, et al. (eds.), *The Vedic Age*, Bombay: Bharatiya Vidya Bhavan, 1951.

[32]Mentioned in E. Bryant, *The Quest for the Origins of Vedic Culture*, New Delhi: Oxford University Press, 2001, p. 276.

not conducive to advancing knowledge as has been argued persuasively by more than one commentator.[33] Nor can the discussion of Vedic origins be reduced to a debate between 'Westerners' and 'Indians' as some would have it. This does the debate an injustice. The theory has been used for all manner of purposes by 'Westerners' and 'Indians' in the past. At least in present times it is possible to demarcate the scholarly from the non-scholarly pursuit, irrespective of whether the person is a 'Westerner' or an 'Indian'. This should be the basis of the debate.

The two main issues on which the debate has focused are chronology and identity. But much else has come under investigation and has resulted in historically stimulating questions. The chronological question has been whittled down largely to the date of the *Rig Veda*. The generally accepted view is that it cannot be dated earlier than about 1500 BCE on linguistic grounds. The names of deities and some Indo–Aryan words in the Mitanni–Hittite treaty of 1380 BCE in Anatolia have linguistic forms that are thought to be more archaic than the *Rig Veda*. The date of the treaty is a useful chronological peg. There are also some words linked to the training of horses. The presence of horses was new to West Asia since they arrived there from Central Asia, at the start of the second millennium BCE, as they did elsewhere in the region. These fragments of Indo–Aryan survived for a brief while and then disappeared when the

---

[33]M. Nanda, *Prophets Facing Backwards: Postmodernism, Science, and Hindu Nationalism*, New Delhi: Permanent Black, 2003.

local languages asserted their dominance. This language cannot have come from India as there is no connecting link, neither archaeological nor linguistic, between India and northern Syria. It has been suggested that it originated in the area between the Caspian Sea and the Oxus.[34]

Another language which is a cognate of the language of the *Rig Veda* is Old Iranian, the language of the *Avesta*, a Zoroastrian text of approximately the same period. The *Avesta* is currently being dated to about 1300 BCE and its language according to some scholars is somewhat more archaic than that of the *Rig Veda*. Apart from language there are also other similarities. Mitra and Varuna are important deities in the *Avesta* as they were in the *Rig Veda*, prior to the ascendance of Indra and Agni. But Indra is not a sympathetic deity in the *Avesta*. Some names and concepts are virtually the same in the two languages although curiously their meanings are often reversed. Thus the Avestan Daeva has the opposite connotation to the Rigvedic Deva. Similarly the Avestan Ahura is the great beneficial spirit although the word is the linguistic counterpart to the Rigvedic Asura. The dual division of the Airiia and the Daha is the equivalent of the Vedic Arya and Dasa. The 's' and the 'h' are interchangeable in the two languages as in parallel geographic names, e.g., Haraxvati/ Sarasvati. The cult of Soma, the hallucinogen that is ritually consumed in the course of some Vedic sacrifices is also important to the *Avesta* and known as

---

[34]T. Burrow, 'The Proto-Indo–Aryans', *Journal of the Royal Asiatic Society*, *Vol. 2*, 1973, pp. 123–40.

Hoama. Interestingly, it does not occur as a ritual in the rites associated with other communities of Indo–European speakers.

Similarities can suggest a closeness of cultures. Both were agro-pastoral societies and primarily cattle-keepers. They show little familiarity with urban centres and the economies of production and exchange associated with such centres. There are no descriptions of monumental structures or the areas of a city such as are associated with urban settlements. Wealth is computed in animals particularly horses and cows. Horses were relatively new to this area which might explain why they are not depicted on the Harappan seals whereas the bull is common. The eating of cattle flesh was restricted to ritual occasions, characteristic of many primarily cattle-herding societies. Migrations are explicitly mentioned in the *Avesta* as well as the direction of the migrations. The reconstruction of the Iranian society of this period would have a bearing on the reconstruction of society across the borderlands in northern India.

By this time, *c.* 1300 BCE, the Indus cities which preceded the *Rig Veda* had declined. If there is an insistence that Indian civilization has to have Aryan foundations then obviously the *Rig Veda* as the earliest evidence of an Aryan presence has to be either prior to or contemporary with the Indus cities. Hence the suggestion that the *Rig Veda* be dated a couple of thousand years earlier than the date accepted so far, and that the language and culture of the Indus cities be taken as Indo–Aryan. But the evidence for this is not forthcoming.

Astronomy has been introduced into the discussion on

the chronology of the *Rig Veda*. Hermann Jacobi argued, a century ago, for an early date on the basis of what he read as references to planetary positions.[35] Modern aids to assess possible astronomical data have been suggested but without arriving at a conclusive date.[36] Recent views have questioned the claim that the Vedic corpus which has references to the Saptarishi/Ursa Major in the far north and the Krittika/Pleiades in the east, were composed in *c.* 3000 BCE.[37] Furthermore, information from much earlier times can get embedded in some channels of continuity from the past, such as ritual, and through this channel continue into later times, as we know from texts of the historical period. Rituals were a major concern of the Vedic compositions and some drew on astronomy. The Indus cities declined but some rituals could well have survived, especially among the Dasi-putra Brahmanas—the Brahmanas who were the sons of Dasis. But this does not date the text to an early period. Evidence from astronomy to date the *Rig Veda* is therefore problematic. The nature of the Rigvedic hymns is such that it is difficult to put them in a chronological order. They are essentially ritual compositions and in some passages deliberately anachronistic.

---

[35]H. Jacobi, 'On the Date of the Rig-Veda', *Indian Antiquary*, 23, 1895, pp.154–59.

[36]B. N. Narahari Achar, 'On Exploring the Vedic Sky with Modern Computer Software', *Electronic Journal of Vedic Studies*, 5, 2, 1999.

[37]M. Witzel, 'The Pleiades and the Bears Viewed from Inside the Vedic Texts', *Electronic Journal of Vedic Studies*, 5.2, 1999; A. Parpola, *Deciphering the Indus Script*, Cambridge: Cambridge University Press, 1994.

Although the re-examination of the evidence from archaeology has resulted in the discarding of the earlier notion of a systematic destruction of Harappan cities by Aryan invaders, this does not automatically lead to the corollary that the speakers of Indo–Aryan were indigenous to India. Indo–Aryan became the dominant language but the historical process by which this happened still needs to be explored. There are enough references in the Vedic corpus to non-Aryan speakers. It was not an isolated language that evolved within the confines of the upper Indus plain. It had close cognates in Iran where it was also dominant and remained so. The links with Old Iranian and the language of the *Avesta* suggest more than just a linguistic affinity with Indo–Aryan. The interaction of peoples, even small groups through their languages and cultures, over a period of time that extends into centuries, brings its own mutations. Small migrations over long durations are not as visible as are massive movements, nevertheless, they can be effective mechanisms of change.

Pastoral circuits for example, can involve large herds of animals, fewer humans but a regularity of contact that could well bring about exchange and bilingualism. Historians have to consider typologies of exchange, migration, technology, and relationships that occur particularly in well-defined regions, such as those on either side of the Indo–Iranian borderlands. Archaeological data can sometimes provide clues to these if stray artefacts suggest exchange or movement. Even if it is argued that Indo–Aryan was indigenous to India, (although the viability of the argument has not been established), the evolution of the language in terms of why it incorporated other linguistic forms from other indigenous languages needs to be explained. Single items in themselves do not necessarily tell us much. A handful of horse bones from various scattered sites do not add up to a culture centred on the horse, as described in the *Rig Veda*.

V

LEADS OF DIFFERENT KINDS

There are many summaries of existing opinions—short and long—and these keep getting repeated without any substantial attempt at considering new perspectives. This might suggest that leads of different kinds should be followed up instead of just the ones we are familiar with. There is a certain creeping ennui now that is associated with 'the Aryan Question'. Its long presence in political debate, has assured it a space in public discourse. However, the new sources and disciplines now contributing to its research are presenting new kinds of questions to the historian. The debate on origins and identities can be investigated through other aspects of the history of this period.

Potentially important recent archaeological discoveries have been the excavations of the Bactria–Margiana Archaeological Complex (BMAC) or what has been called the Oxus Civilization, stretching from the Caspian to the Pamirs and active in the period from 2300–1900 but less active in the subsequent period until 1500 BCE.[38] The BMAC

---

[38] V. I. Sarianidi, 'Near Eastern Aryans in Central Asia', *The Journal of*

at an early crossroads of Asia had links with the Iranian plateau, Baluchistan, the Indus borderlands, and the steppes of Central Asia. It was partly contemporary with the period of the Harappan cities and had its own urban centres in its oases. Were the items exchanged items of trade or were they items of gift exchange, or some of each, since either would make a difference to the nature of the relationships involved in the exchange? Connections are also attested by the location of a Harappan settlement at Shortughai in the Pamirs, known as a source of lapis lazuli that was presumably exported to Mesopotamia. The period of decline of the BMAC coincides interestingly with the decline of Harappan urbanism and with changes in the wider area that had earlier been linked. Despite its proximity to cultures thought to have been Indo–European speaking, it remains unclear whether the BMAC used an Indo–European language since written records have not been found.

The decline in exchange between the urban centres may encourage one to think of a more marked presence of agro-pastoralists—a pattern not unfamiliar to later history.[39] Their

---

Indo-European Studies, 27, 1999, pp. 3–4, 295–326; H-P Francfort, 'La civilisation de l'Oxus et les Indo-Iraniens et Indo-Aryens', in G. Fussman et al. (eds), *Aryas, Aryens et Iraniens en Asie Centrale*, Paris: Institut Civilisation Indienne, 2005, pp. 253–328; P. T. Hiebert, *Origins of the Bronze Age Oasis Civilisation in Central Asia*, Cambridge, Massachusetts: Harvard University Press, 1994.

[39]G. Fussman, 'Entre fantasmes, science et politique: l'entrée des Aryas en Inde', in G. Fussman et al. (eds.), *Aryas, Aryens et Iraniens en Asie Centrale*, Paris: Institut Civilisation Indienne, 2005, pp. 197–232.

presence is evident from textual sources dating to the period when the BMAC was not so active. The Gatha sections of the *Avesta* are now said to be earlier than had been assumed[40] with a date of the mid-second millennium BCE or soon thereafter. There are some echoes of what are said to be the earlier migrations of peoples and perhaps languages in later Avestan sections with references to the lands created by Ahura Mazda and associated with the Airiia. These are listed from the northernmost, Airiianem Vaego, coming south to Helmand and still further to Hapta Hindhu/Sapta Sindhu and its vicinity.[41] The list of places suggests a migratory route from perhaps the Oxus region to the borderlands and then to the Indus region. There appears to have been a memory of a migration.

Pastoral groups may have been part of a Central Asian cultural nexus which in the course of segmenting and moving also manifested local differences. The widening of pastoral circuits and the resulting interface with new societies and cultures would have affected the forms and structures of the earlier society. Ecological similarities would have encouraged diffusion but unfamiliar environments would have created some diversity. What were the factors that encouraged the widening of the pastoral circuits, if that is what happened? Was it a search for pastures and fresh water sources in a

---

[40]J. Kellens, 'Les *airiia*–ne sont pas des Aryas: ce sont deja des Iraniens', in G. Fussman et.al. (eds.), *Aryas, Aryens et Iraniens en Asie Centrale*, Paris, 2005, pp. 233–52.

[41]James Darmesteter, (trans.), *The Zend-Avesta, Part I, The Vendidad*, Oxford: Clarendon Press, 1883, 1.4.

possible period of drought as has been suggested? Was it a demographic alteration? The relations between the societies of the *Avesta* and the *Rig Veda* can be meaningfully explored to search for answers to such questions as can the archaeology of the regions familiar to these societies.

As has been said, that there were no political borders in those days and movements across geographical borderlands were not controlled by political boundaries. The boundary of the territories of British India cannot be the criterion for what is indigenous and what is alien to India. The presence of material objects in the archaeological record and their chronologies and distribution define cultures, as do the linguistic structure of the languages of the texts and the geographical direction taken by language and textual sources. Non-Indo–Aryan linguistic forms in the *Rig Veda*[42] register contact between speakers of various languages. The types of linguistic importations could point to activities associated with specific languages and their speakers. It was suggested that tools used in agriculture tend to come from non-Indo–Aryan languages, such as Dravidian or/and Austro-Asiatic.[43] A fuller investigation of this might provide some worthwhile explanations of the social interface.

---

[42]M. M. Deshpande, 'Genesis of Rigvedic Retroflexion', in M. M. Deshpande and P. Hook (eds.), *Aryan and Non-Aryan in India*, Ann Arbor: University of Michigan, Centre for South and Southeast Asian Studies, 1979; F. B. J. Kuiper, *Aryans in the Rigveda*, Amsterdam: Editions Rodopi, 1991.

[43]T. Burrow, 'The Proto-Indo–Aryans', *Journal of the Royal Asiatic Society*, *Vol. 2*, 1973, p. 373 ff; F. B. J. Kuiper, *Aryans in the Rigveda*, Amsterdam: Editions Rodopi, 1991.

There needs to be a more precise definition of concepts such as chiefships and kingships as applied to the history of these times. The activities of the raja in the *Rig Veda*, for instance, agree more closely with those of a chief of the clan rather than a king. The popular assemblies associated with chiefships such as samitis and vidathas are not characteristic institutions of kingship; the sabhas of kingship were different.[44] The differentiation can also be sought in the sites where material culture could indicate differences. Urbanism is a distinctive change from previous settlements. Proof of urbanism requires evidence of many aspects of its functions—economic, administrative, and social to say the least—as is apparent from the excavations of the Harappan cities. As has been argued it is incorrect to maintain that the word pur/a stockade as it occurs in the *Rig Veda* has the same meaning as the pura/a town in later texts.

Sharpening definitions of forms of authority would require other data such as the juxtaposition of pastoralism and agriculture and the nature of reciprocal exchange. Did the juxtaposition, for instance, in places where the pastoralists and the farmers had a symbiotic relationship as seen in animal herds grazing on the harvest stubble, bring about the borrowing of linguistic features from one language to another? Chiefdoms rely more on exchange of various kinds being reciprocal where items exchanged need not be identical

---

[44]Romila Thapar, *From Lineage to State*, New Delhi: Oxford University Press, 1984; '*Rigveda*: Encapsulating Social Change', in K. N. Panikkar et al. (eds.), *The Making of History*, Delhi: Manohar, 2000, pp. 11–40.

but their evaluation is seen as equivalent. Kingdoms tend to rely more on nurturing dominant groups which help in controlling subordinate groups. The hierarchy of power is more complex. The seemingly egalitarian distribution of booty among clansmen after a raid, with some concession to a more substantial share for the priest and the raja, would be gradually replaced by the inequities of the induction of labour to ensure an income for the chief. This would change the nature of relationships. A statement such as, the kshatr/personifying power, eats the vish/the clansmen, in the same way as the deer eats grain, is obviously saying something about the system of control and not merely making a comparison (*Shatapatha Brahmana*, 8.7.1.2., 8.7.2.2., 9.4.3.5.). Monitoring changes such as these could be correlated with change in language or material culture.

The historical reconstruction of this period now presents a different picture from earlier theories. The identification of archaeological cultures as 'Aryan' without the evidence of writing was methodologically doubtful and has now become more so. To make direct correlation between language and archaeological artefacts is problematic, although there can be parallels between objects mentioned in texts and those found in excavations. Even in periods when the languages of dispersed areas are related, as in the case of Indo–Aryan in northern India and its cognates in Anatolia and north-east Iran, the material culture of the societies speaking these languages is dissimilar.

The notion of an Aryan race was enhanced in the past by reference to the use of an Aryan language. The notion of an

Aryan race has been discarded for over fifty years. Language and race are distinctly different categories. It would be more correct to use the label of Indo–Aryan when referring to the language, and to use Aryan as Arya, as it was used in the past, to qualify those observing certain social and linguistic norms. The overlay of nineteenth century theories and the more generalized current debates has merely confused its usage. How and when the Indo–Aryan language became current in the upper Indus plain now requires investigation in the context of the linguistic forms that it has incorporated from other contemporary language groups. These are forms that exist only in Indo–Aryan and not in the other languages with which it was most closely associated in Iran and Anatolia.[45] Had Indo–Aryan spread from the Punjab to Iran and Anatolia, then these borrowings should have been present in the language of the *Avesta* and the Mitanni–Hittite treaty.[46] The spread of the Indo–Aryan language was a continuing process in Indian history. Within the subcontinent it was used in addition to local languages. Where some elements of the latter were inducted this could provide clues to the earlier process. The links and connections between societies across the Indo–Iranian borderlands could be examined through the

---

[45]M. B. Emeneau, 'Linguistic Prehistory of India', in *Proceedings of the American Philosophical Society*, 98, 1954, pp. 282–92; M. A. Mehendale, 'Indo–Aryans, Indo–Iranians and Indo–Europeans', in S. B. Deo and S. Kamath (eds.), *The Aryan Problem*, Pune: Bharatiya Itihasa Sankalana Samiti, 1993, pp. 43–50.

[46]J. P. Mallory, *In Search of the Indo–Europeans*, London: Thames & Hudson, 1989.

evidence of artifacts travelling distances as well as linguistic changes among those using related languages.

This would suggest that we look for a graduated interaction over some centuries among the players who created these societies and cultures. There is little evidence for large-scale violent conflict and warfare despite the Harappan cities being fortified. Why were elaborate fortifications necessary or was it assumed that they were somehow necessary in the evolution of urbanism? The subsequent *Rig Veda* describes inter-clan hostility, but on a small scale, sometimes among the Arya clans and sometimes between the Aryas and the Dasas. Arya priests on occasion performed rituals for Dasa chiefs such as Bribu and Balbutha even if the traditional worship of the latter was different. The nature of these relationships needs to be fine-tuned. Texts on ritual exegesis associated with the *Rig Veda* refer with respect even to those Brahmanas who were the sons of Dasa women. This would query the simplistic understanding of caste as varna, applying the norms of the later *Dharmashastras* to earlier times. It would seem that the relationship was more ambivalent than has been granted so far.[47] The adoption of those outside the social pale such as the sons of Dasis into Brahmana caste status also contradicts previous notions of caste exclusiveness (*Aitareya Brahmana* 7.18).

---

[47]D. D. Kosambi, 'On the Origin of Brahmin Gotras', 1950, reprinted in Brajadulal Chattopadhyaya, ed., *The Oxford India Kosambi: Combined Methods in Indology and Other writings*, New Delhi: Oxford University Press, 2002, pp. 98-166; 'Rigveda: Encapsulating Social Change', in K. N. Panikkar et al. (eds.), *The Making of History*, Delhi: Manohar, 2000.

The centrality of the Vedic texts for later history has been largely treated as the continuity of ritual and belief systems. As religious texts they were highly respected in some upper caste circles and said to be divine revelations, whereas others even of the upper castes, such as the Shramana sects did not take them to be so. From the early centuries CE, the popularity of Puranic Hinduism, whose texts were the Puranas which introduced rituals and belief systems from various other sources as well, superseded the centrality of the Vedas except among the topmost caste. For some religious exponents and philosophers and their followings such as those of the Shramanic sects of Buddhists, Jainas, Ajivikas, Carvakas, and such like, the Vedas had been one among the starting points of intellectual questioning, and of disagreement with Vedic Brahmanism, leading to different beliefs and practice. This continued through the centuries with lively confrontations, some compromises and some vitriolic exchange.

The evidence of social change in these texts has received less attention. Why some clans and castes came to dominate society and others were subordinated in this period, have implications for social history. Hierarchies, differentiations and regulations are part of the social process in complex societies and evolve in localized exchanges. They cannot be explained away merely by resort to the presence of conquerors as they were in earlier studies nor by the societies being described as uniformly and universally harmonious. Local hierarchies also undergo mutation. But when there is an insistence on making a system universal, such as the imposition of caste rules over extensive areas, then it has to be assumed that this reflects historical change of a substantial kind, involving a diversity of groups not all of whom were in agreement. Where a range of groups have to be incorporated into positions of status, their ethnic origins may well have been set aside in favour of imposing a language and social norms. Language, inherited or learnt, would be a crucial indicator. Notions of what is indigenous and what is alien are neither permanent nor unchanging nor transparent. The identities of the indigenous and the alien constantly mutate throughout history and the mutation indicates a historical change.

The Vedas when treated as sources of history have to be subjected to the same analyses as all other sources. They are questioned in terms of who composed them, for what purpose, whose views do they reflect, whose do they condemn and so on. It is significant that the hymns of the *Rig Veda* as we have them now, in the recension of Shakalya, were not at all composed at the same time but over a few centuries. Therefore, some change would be registered in the context of the early hymns as compared to the later. Social history would involve investigating the organization of the various groups referred to as well as their rituals, technologies and economies. Merely listing items mentioned is not enough, for it requires an assessment of the broader frameworks of social and economic functioning.

The emphasis on defining a particular kind of Aryanism as foundational to Indian civilization is not an indigenous interpretation of history as is claimed. As we have seen, it is a revival of certain trends in nineteenth century colonial historiography but now moulded by the more specific ideological concerns of contemporary politics and society. In the past the theory has been used by many as an agency of empowerment and entitlement to include some and exclude others. This in itself cannot be curtailed since resort to history—particularly ancient history—has been part of the agenda of various nationalisms and imperialisms and continues to be so in some cases. Nevertheless, historians, archaeologists, specialists in linguistics and in other disciplines that bear on the subject, need to be constantly in a scholarly dialogue so as to assess the validity of the theories being suggested. Such verifications are also signposts for the interested general reader.

VI

THEORIES CURRENTLY OF PUBLIC INTEREST

The Hindutva version of the theory, formulated in the 1920s and 30s, glossed over the question of an invasion when referring to the Aryans as having settled in northern India but emphasized their distinctiveness and role as the progenitors of the Hindu and of Hinduism. This facilitated endorsing the indigenous origins of the Aryans and their culture which followed closely as a theory. Living in the Sindhu/Indus plain welded them into a nation and gave them the name of Hindu, derived from Sindhu. There was an insistence on a homeland within the Indian subcontinent. Since India was the homeland of the Aryans, Aryan civilization travelled from India to the West. All Hindus are members of the Aryan race, and therefore are not aliens. Hindus are united by the bonds of common blood, the blood of the mighty race, incorporated with and descended from the Vedic forefathers.[48] Drawing on nineteenth century colonial ideas of race, it was said that the Race-Spirit of the Hindus did not die out and enabled the Hindus to defend themselves against 'the murdering hordes of Mussalman freebooters'.[49] The constituents of a nation are the territory hereditarily occupied, race, religion and culture which create the Race-Spirit, and language.[50] Those who do not belong to the Hindu nation cannot live in India except as foreigners unless they agree to be 'naturalized', namely, discard their previous religion, culture and language.

This view is clear about what constitutes the Indian/Hindu identity. As I have mentioned earlier, Savarkar maintained that an Indian/Hindu is one for whom India is his Pitribhumi and his Punyabhumi, the land of his ancestors and the land where his religion originated. This definition of the Indian as Hindu effectively cut out the Muslims and the Christians which was intentional according to the text, and to this was also added the Communists for good measure! There is, therefore, a confusion of the categories involved—that of race, religion and ideology. The link between these views and the beginnings of Indian history is that they have become influential in popular versions of history, and the demands of political ideology have

[48]V. D. Savarkar, *Hindutva: Who is a Hindu?*, Bombay: Veer Savarkar Prakashan, 1922, p.68.
[49]M. S. Golwalkar, *We, Or Our Nationhood Defined*, Nagpur: Bharat Publications, 1938, p. 10.
[50]Ibid., 18 ff; 28 ff.

led to attempts to change school textbooks in order to give the Hindutva interpretation of history.

The concept of the Hindu Arya created problems in relation to what the colonial administration called Scheduled Castes. Whether these groups constituted Hindu Aryas or not was debated among caste Hindus. The more orthodox supporters of Hindutva were for excluding them, but when the game of numbers was seen as important to elections, there was a move to incorporate the Scheduled Castes as Hindus and thus swell the numbers of the Hindus. Reference was made by some to the common blood of all Hindus from the Brahmana to the Chandala.[51] But the issue remained somewhat confused because Golwalkar returned to the concept of the Race-Spirit[52] inspired by Nazi Germany, although his actual intention was the separating of Hindu and Muslim. Common blood and the purity of race allowed for a separate Hindu identity. But the problem remained, for if the Aryans incorporated the non-Aryans then it could be argued that this had interfered with racial purity.

The theory had to be changed from that of Jyotiba Phule in order to claim the antiquity and continuity of the Hindu Rashtra and to provide a different identity to the Hindu, distinct from Indians following other religions. For Phule, the Aryan Brahmana was 'the Other'. In the Hindutva version it is the non-Aryan and the non-Hindu.[53] This is a significant

---

[51]Savarkar, *Hindutva: Who is a Hindu?*, p. 89.
[52]Golwalkar, *We, Or Our Nationhood Defined*, pp. 39–40.
[53]Ibid., 18 ff; 28 ff.

shift from caste to religion. But neither of these two versions was initially hegemonic.

The earlier mainstream version deriving again from the nineteenth century and from Max Müller, was attractive to many upper-caste middle-class Hindus. This version held that there was an Aryan invasion and that the Aryans, speaking Indo–Aryan or Vedic Sanskrit, conquered the indigenous population, culturally and racially distinct from the superior Aryan. Support for this theory took some rather emphatic forms. Max Müller and Muir had maintained that upper caste Hindus were the biological, lineal descendants of the Aryans. The claim to kinship ties with the British based on the Aryan connection became an attempt at self-promotion by upper caste Hindus.[54]

Yet others with a more nationalist opinion had a different reading. Dayanand Saraswati propagated a return to the Vedas as the source of Indian civilization. The purity of Sanskrit was insisted upon and has contributed to a suspicion of modern linguistics which does not endorse this purity. B. G. Tilak had little time for the views of Phule. For him the coming of the Aryans was a positive development in Indian history.

Here the theory was closely tied to nationalism and was used to strengthen the status of the upper castes from which there came the new middle-class professionals. There was now an implicit inching towards a class utilization of the

[54]K. C. Sen, *Keshub Chunder Sen's Lectures in India*, London: Cassell and Company, Limited, 1904.

theory to support the superiority of the emergent midd
class. There is little or no attempt to even dismiss Phul
reading that the invasion led to the oppression of the low
castes.

The concept of race was alien, hence the word wa
translated inappropriately as jati. The choice was probabl
determined by the circular argument that caste was racia
segregation. Although the word jati is linked to birth, the
identification of jatis is also drawn from a variety of social
and religious activities that can change the constituents of jati
identity. The recognition of intermarriage among jatis would
also militate against its being defined as race, as does the fact
that some jatis are constantly incorporating and creating new
jatis. Caste had been frequently contested in history but with
other markers such as language, occupation, and sect, had
been continually redefined. But when race was introduced
into this contestation some projected it as the most 'scientific'
of the markers.

The history of social change within a caste-based society
was given little attention by earlier historians, many of whom
were content to project the frozen nature of caste. With
language and caste both being linked to racial identities,
cultural history was frequently explained in terms of the
spread of the Aryan race and its culture, monitored by
the presence of Brahmanical belief and practice. A gradual
departure from this general assessment of the impact of the
Aryans was the realization by culture—historians, sociologists
and anthropologists, and some studying Indian religion, that
there was more than upper caste Aryanism in the making of

Indian history and civilization.[55] This was also an attempt to broaden the base of nationalist inclusive history.

VII

INTERPRETATIONS OF THE THEORY

The variant interpretations of the Aryan theory illustrate its role in the political agendas of various social groups and the nature of the contestation between these groups. It reflects therefore what has been called the organizing capacity of intellectual rationalizations in the form of theories of fictive ethnicity.[56] Appeal to a seemingly scientific explanation of biological heredity is made to coincide with racial categories. It provides nationalist myths of selective linear history in which the genetic descent of a 'nation' is sought to be traced and authority comes naturally to those of the upper castes or of the dominant religion; or alternatively a demand is made for the restitution of the rights of those who see themselves as having been denied their claims to being the inheritors of the land. Racism presupposes a fear of bastardization and underlines separateness. It is at the same time intelligible to large numbers and touches on commonly felt insecurities. It has also endorsed sub-nationalist identity myths, again identifying religion or language with race.

For a few decades the theory received less attention, perhaps because the earlier linear historical narrative had

---

[55]N. K. Bose, 'Caste in India', *Man in India*, 1951, 31, 3–4, pp. 107–23; G. S. Ghurye, *Vedic India*, Delhi: Popular Prakashan, 1979; I. Karve, *Kinship Organisation in India*, Delhi: Munshiram Manoharlal, 1961.
[56]E. Balibar and I. Wallerstein, *Race, Nation, Class*, London: Verso, 1991.

been shaken up by the newly discovered archaeological evidence of the Indus Civilization. This evidence had to be incorporated into the theory, and accommodated to the evidence of the Vedic corpus, creating a new problem since the two sources were not compatible. Indo–European language studies were more generally beginning to introduce archaeological evidence in the reconstruction of societies said to be using Indo–European languages. As has been noted, the discovery of the Indus Civilization raised pertinent questions regarding the Aryan beginnings of Indian history. There was of course the inevitable search for the Aryans in archaeological evidence and for a while every new archaeological culture dating to a period between 2000–1000 BCE tended to be labelled as 'Aryan'. In a sense, the fashion had been set by Gordon Childe, but without his caveats, it became a wild goose chase. Cautioning against equating archaeological cultures with languages in the absence of a deciphered script was generally ignored.

The foremost of the obstacles posed by the archaeological data was the existence of the urban Harappan civilization familiar with written communication, which was prior to the Vedic sources and very different in culture from the Vedic; and equally important, what appeared to be the absence of evidence of any large-scale invasion during this period. Such a change in evidence was problematic for all the accepted theories.

The development of Harappan urban centres in northern and western India observed a similarity of cultural form which is distinctively different from the diversity of pre-

Harappan cultures each limited to a particular region.[57] The Harappan cities used these as a base although the process of urbanization seems to have had its genesis in the Indus plain itself in about 2700 BCE. Harappan cities began to decline by the early or mid-second millennium BCE, but some of the smaller settlements continued and then petered out or else were mutated through contact with other locally evolved cultures. A few of these have evidence of contemporaneity between the late Harappan and the subsequent culture, such as the Black-and-Red Ware in Gujarat, or an overlap at a few sites of the Painted Grey Ware (PGW) and Late Harappan in the Punjab. Some continuities, albeit extremely limited, can therefore be posited between the Harappan and post-Harappan cultures.

New cultures emerge at various places by the end of the second millennium as in the Swat Valley, Baluchistan, Gujarat, Punjab, Rajasthan and the Ganga Valley, but have their own individual and recognizably different characteristics. There is more than a hint of continuing contacts across the Indo–Iranian borderlands. The question then relates to the authorship of the new items which surface as a result of these contacts.

The questioning of the theory of an Aryan invasion arose from the paucity of archaeological evidence suggesting such an invasion. There is occasional evidence of what might be

---

[57]F. R. Allchin, ed., *The Archaeology of Early Historic South Asia*, Cambridge: Cambridge University Press, 1995; D. K. Chakrabarti, *The Archaeology of Ancient Indian Cities*, New Delhi: Oxford University Press, 1995.

reconstructed as an attack on a site. Skirmishes and local conflicts can be expected, especially in areas where there was a search for new pastures and water resources. But there was no replacement on a large scale of local cultures by an intruding culture or the destruction of sites systematically over a sizeable area.

Archaeologists supporting the Hindutva view maintain that the Indus Civilization should be renamed the Indus–Sarasvati Civilization, because of a large number of pre- and Mature Harappan sites clustered in Cholistan in the third millennium BC. This part of the Hakra River was identified by some with the Sarasvati as mentioned in the *Rig Veda*.[58] Changing the name attempts to capture the Indus Civilization for India and more so for Vedic India and emphasizes Vedic links, since the Sarasvati River is lauded in the *Rig Veda*. It also reflects the priority given to territory as the basis of the Hindu Arya identity where it reached out to the subcontinent and most particularly to the northwest. The original homeland—Sindhusthan, or the Indus plain—now in present-day Pakistan, makes that the area for the foundational civilization. That the insistence is on calling it Indus–Sarasvati rather than perhaps what might be the geographically more appropriate Indus–Hakra, should the contribution of the Hakra valley be regarded as essential, also points to the intention in changing the name.

---

[58]S. P. Gupta, 'Longer Chronology of the Indus Sarasvati Civilisation', *Puratattva*, 1992-93, 23, pp. 21–29; V. N. Misra, 'Indus Civilisation and the Rigvedic Sarasvati', in A. Parpola et al. *South Asian Archaeology* 1993, Vol. II, Helsinki, 1994.

Not surprisingly the Hindutva arguments generally ignore the linguistic analyses of Vedic Sanskrit, which had established it as part of the wider Indo–European family with cognates in Old Iranian. G. A. Grierson's *Linguistic Survey of India* dominated the study of Indian languages, and the history of language in India was seen largely in terms of the spread of Indo–Aryan. Now it is being argued that there are non-Aryan linguistic components in Indo–Aryan even as early as the *Rig Veda*.[59] One view describes some elements as linguistic convergence.[60] This would question equating the identity of race and language among 'Vedic Aryans'.

The monitoring of non-Aryan in Vedic Sanskrit provides an interesting pattern. Non-Aryan linguistic elements are present in the *Rig Veda* but the presence is stronger with the migration in geographical location from the Punjab to the Ganga plain, a shift which is evident from the distribution of the dialects of Indo–Aryan in the Vedic corpus[61] and the occasional reference in the Vedas to migrations eastwards such as the much quoted migration of Videgha Mathava. The archaeological picture of the Ganga plain indicates that it was

---

[59]F. B. J. Kuiper, *Aryans in the Rigveda*, Amsterdam: Editions Rodopi, 1991; M. B. Emeneau, 'Linguistic Prehistory of India', in *Proceedings of the American Philosophical Society*, 98, 1954, pp. 282–92, Burrow, *The Sanskrit Language*, London: Faber and Faber, 1965.

[60]H. H. Hock, 'Subversion or Convergence? The Issue of Pre-Vedic Retroflexion Re-examined', in *Studies in the Linguistic Sciences*, 1993, 23, 2, pp. 74–109.

[61]M. Witzel, 'Tracing the Vedic Dialects', in C. Caillat, ed., *Dialectes dans les Litteratures Indo-Aryennes*, Paris, 1989, p. 97 ff.

peopled with earlier settlements with whom those coming from the Indo–Gangetic watershed would have had to make adjustments. A case in point is the spread of the Painted Grey Ware culture into the Doab where it occupied sites close to those of the earlier Ochre Colour Pottery culture and those of the Black-and-Red Ware cultures.[62] It is not necessary to identify any single one of these cultures with 'the Aryans', but there is an interaction between these cultures which may be reflected in the evolution of the language of the Indo–Aryan speakers as recorded in the later Vedic corpus. Not only is there a borrowing of some vocabulary, as for example words relating to agricultural processes, but also the currency of morphological and phonetic forms and syntax from Dravidian and Austro-Asiatic languages. This was a mixing of at least two distinctive language systems, the agglutinative Dravidian and the inflectional Indo–Aryan. This has reinforced the theory that the speakers of Indo–Aryan migrated into northern India and settled among non-Aryan speakers, with the use of two languages perhaps leading to a long period of bilingualism. This may account for the presence of non-Aryan in Vedic Sanskrit.[63] Differences in Vedic dialects and the emergence of a variety of Prakrits by the middle of the first millennium would also suggest a mingling of the speakers of various languages, quite apart from the changes resulting from the

---

[62]T. N. Roy, *The Ganges Civilisation*, New Delhi: Ramanand Vidya Bhawan, 1983.

[63]M. B. Emeneau, 'Linguistic Prehistory of India', in *Proceedings of the American Philosophical Society*, 98, 1954.

natural evolution of the language.

The replacing of invasion by migration as discussed by many archaeologists and historians, raises another set of questions. The historian has to explain how the language entered India and came to be established as the language of the elite. Languages come with people but those that speak the same language need not be racially the same. The spread of a language does not have to be linked to overwhelming numbers of people. The process of language change can be achieved if other factors relating to the historical context encourage it. If there is an insistence that Indo–Aryan evolved within India and without any contact with other regions, then its linguistic prehistory will have to be demonstrated to show the process of evolution in isolation to the point where it becomes Vedic Sanskrit.

Archaeology, in the absence of inscriptions, cannot provide the evidence for a language or for a change of language. But it can provide the evidence for the presence and location of various cultures, for the contacts between societies, and for a broad delineation of their social and economic systems. The geographical area under discussion has to be demarcated and differentiated. The characteristics of the borderlands and the Punjab were substantially different from those of the middle Ganga plain, or for that matter of the Vindhyas and adjoining areas.

On the basis of some coming and going across the Indo–Iranian borderlands, judging by the presence of artefacts in different areas, it seems that there may have been small-scale migrations motivated by pastoralism and incipient trade, both of which were well-established activities from earlier times. Migrations and the interchange of language in these areas have been a constant feature of its history over the millennia. In the course of such movements it is possible that pastoral clans with a mobile segment using horses, began to negotiate alliances with the settlements which had survived the economic collapse of the Harappan system. Or this could have been the background to a symbiotic relationship between pastoralists and agriculturalists, frequent in the subcontinent until recently. Pastoralists bring their herds to graze on the stubble of the harvested crops of the agriculturalists, to the advantage of both. The stubble provides natural feed for the animals and the animals in turn fertilize the fields with their droppings. Such an arrangement if carried out regularly, would automatically lead to much linguistic and cultural interactions. This might explain the multiplicity of words linked to cattle and horses being more often Indo–Aryan, and those linked to agriculture sometimes being initially non-Aryan.

Where there are local predators, there protectors would have the advantage. This advantage did not depend solely on conquest or coercive dominance. It would have involved skirmishes and raids of the kind which are referred to in the *Rig Veda* as also negotiations and alliances and a slow process of interaction with the existing populations. The latter may have resulted in groups which fissioned. Their culture would be far more mixed and distanced from the original migrants. Such processes take their own time and it is not surprising that the change in geographical location and the linguistic changes from the *Rig Veda* to the later Vedic corpus took more than half a millennium. The conflicts referred to in the Vedic corpus can better be viewed from a historical perspective as between various social groups, pastoralists and peasants. But even these were not clearly demarcated and there were many overlapping forms.

As I have said at the beginning of this essay, the attempt at identifying Aryans and the narration of the beginnings of Indian history remain complex problems because they still carry, at the popular level, the baggage of nineteenth century European preconceptions, even if in the European context this baggage has now been rejected as a nineteenth century myth.[64] It has overwhelmed popular renderings of Indian history whereas actually it is not so central. It is now less central to a nationalist reconstruction of the past, although the Hindutva version claims it as crucial to its own form of nationalism. Therefore those who disagree are dubbed anti-national. But continuity lies in what is now its real function and that is political. The crux of the public debate is the crisis of identity and status in the claims to political and social power and a contestation over what is viewed as alternative forms of national culture and ethnic homogeneity.

Parallel to this contemporary political projection of the ancient Arya is the very different current historical research

---

[64]Léon Poliakov, *The Aryan Myth: A History of Racist and Nationalist Ideas in Europe*, (Trans.) Edmund Howard, New York: Basic Books, 1974; E. Leach, 'Aryan Invasions over four Millennia', in E. Ohnuki-Tierney, ed., *Culture Through Time: Anthropological Approaches*, Stanford: Stanford University Press, 1990.

that is revealing fresh aspects of the history of this period. Historians are well aware of the political manipulations of various aspects of this theory. These they have set aside. There has been for the past half century a move away from the colonial reading of the nineteenth century, now regarded as faulty, as well as the subsequent twentieth century interpretations from the perspective of various facets of European racism or local nationalism. The objection is not to explanations changing. On the contrary such changes are expected with the discovery of new sources of knowledge and new methods of enquiry.

The time has come to stay with the evidence as it surfaces and to reposition the argument if necessary. This can come from a variety of sources as is evident in studies of the period—from reading the texts and questioning them, from philological perspectives, from analyses of a linguistic nature, and as more recently, from those sciences that can have a bearing on the history of the period. Among these the most widely discussed currently is genetics. As long as the information is kept clear of controls by a range of bodies that look upon themselves as having the authority to control knowledge, the new investigations could provide additional sources of precise information. The challenge then is to correlate all the diverse information and present a coherent view of the period and one that is generally regarded as reliable by scholars.

IN THE AFTERMATH OF THE HARAPPAN PERIOD (*c.* 2000–500 BCE)

JAYA MENON

Within the ambit of this book which takes a fresh look at the 'Which of Us Are Aryans?' issue, this essay aims to locate the issue archaeologically, in terms of people, their settlements, and their ways of life. To do this, it becomes necessary to flesh out the various archaeological cultures that occupied the chronological space of over a millennium, that is, the period from about 2000–500 BCE. This would then include the late stages of the Harappan, the chalcolithic cultures after the Harappan,[1] and the Iron Age/Painted Grey Ware (PGW), in that chronological order. Roughly, the Harappan period is dated to between 2600 and 1900 BCE, with the later chalcolithic from 1900 to 1500 BCE, and the early Iron Age from 1500 till 500 BCE. The attributions of such terms do not just rest on chronology or, for that matter, geography; rather, it is the nature of the archaeological evidence that are used to mark these apart. Here, we will attempt to understand the archaeological evidence and the main features of this period.

---

[1] The chalcolithic is an archaeological term used for a period when both stone and copper were used.

94

THE HARAPPAN CULTURE

What has popularly been called the Indus Valley Civilization or the Harappan Civilization, or as archaeologists call it, the Mature Harappan or the Harappan culture, belongs to the Bronze Age. This term refers to a period when an alloy of copper and tin were used to make a material out of which the major cutting implements were fashioned. More important, the two metals were, because of their rarity, not easy to procure, and this meant that the Harappans had to travel to obtain the required metals and other materials, or develop networks to bring these materials to them. Other well-known Bronze Age societies, though earlier in date, were the Mesopotamian and the Egyptian, with the common feature of all three being their urban nature. In contrast to other Bronze Age societies, the Harappan is known only archaeologically and not through written evidence, as its inscribed material has not yet been deciphered. Thus, to understand the Harappan and the ways of life of its people, we have to solely depend on material evidence.

We are, then, able to 'identify' the Harappan through a set of material artefacts and the characteristics of these artefacts. These are understood to include, among other things, a red slipped pottery with black designs, metal tools of certain kinds, steatite seals, chert weights, carnelian beads with particular designs, as well as bricks made in a particular ratio of length to breadth to width. Briefly, in archaeological terms, such distinctive artefacts are considered to comprise a 'culture'.[2] The Mature Harappan was sandwiched by chalcolithic 'cultures' that are sometimes called early and late Harappan. It is also precisely the absence and presence of these distinctive artefacts signalling urban characteristics that are used to differentiate chalcolithic cultures prior to and after the Mature Harappan.[3]

The Mature Harappan period or the urban period lasted for roughly 700 years. Those 700 years would have seen periods of intermittent upheaval as suggested by the periodic floods that ravaged Mohenjodaro, a major archaeological site in Sind. After 1900 BCE, however, most of the major sites were abandoned or were clearly in stress, or showed the collapse of civic order. At Mohenjodaro, signs of stress are skeletons in a street (called by excavators 'Deadman Lane') and down the steps in a room with a well. Signs of disorder are encroachments on the previously well-maintained streets. It is not as if the area was completely depopulated or abandoned. On the contrary, several sites continued to exist albeit with an altered material culture. How do we account for the decline of urban societies in the beginning of the second millennium BCE?

A very early theory going back to the 1940s was that the

---

[2]Archaeologists use the word 'culture' where sites and occupations at sites are distinguished on the basis of material traits: certain types and designs on ceramics, tool types, or ornaments. These material traits should be found from a distinct geographical area and period of time in order to qualify to be part of a 'culture'.

[3]Thus, chalcolithic cultures prior to the Mature Harappan are sometimes called pre-urban, and those following, as post-urban.

Aryans or an Aryan invasion was responsible for the decline of the Harappan cities. This has been rejected due to the lack of evidence for military activity or large-scale destruction at Harappan cities. Another pervasive way of looking at Harappan decline has been to blame environmental causes, such as deforestation, earthquakes, excessive floods, and shifts in river courses. Even while some of these factors were pertinent to certain regions, none can account for the decline of the entire civilization. Thus, while river shifts may have impacted sites in the Cholistan region, this would have been irrelevant to sites along the Indus. While certain scholars have attributed Harappan decline to the end of long-distance trading contacts with West Asia, others have suggested that structural issues of a socio-political nature wrought an inability of the Harappan civilization to survive longer.

THE AFTERMATH OF THE MATURE HARAPPAN

An Overview of the Cultures

The prime focus of this essay is, more specifically, the aftermath of the Harappan period. This is a period that sees the re-emergence of chalcolithic societies followed by Iron Age communities. In Baluchistan, there seems to be evidence of destruction at sites. Cemeteries reveal interesting evidence such as copper stamp seals, a shaft-hole axe and painted grey ceramics. On the fringes of the Indus plains, there are graves, some with terracotta figures of horses and horse bones, others with ceramics, and bronze objects including a shaft-hole axe-adze. At Pirak, an important site, a brief Harappan occupation is followed by a desertion of the site and then by an occupation from about 1700 BCE. The ceramics are coarse and artefacts include clay and terracotta figurines of horses and camels with bones of both animals. There is a gradual increase of the latter type of artefacts over time along with the introduction of figurines of the Bactrian camel. By about 1370 BCE, the first iron is recorded at the site.

In the region of Gandhara, a number of cemeteries with distinctive grave goods were investigated and have been called 'Gandhara Grave culture'. Chronologically, they cover a long period from 1500 to 200 BCE. Burials are in pits with stone used for walls and roof. Burials have complete skeletons, as also collected bones, and there is some evidence of cremation. The ceramics are plain pottery in buff-red or grey. Metal objects are largely of copper or bronze and rarely of iron. There are also two horse burials in separate graves, and a bronze model of a horse. B. Allchin and R. Allchin[4] suggest looking to the Caucasus, north Iran, and Central Asia for parallels for these graves.

In the Harappan region, the aftermath is marked by a general disintegration of ways of urban living and the collapse of planning that distinguished Harappan cities. At sites that continue to show chalcolithic occupation, these later levels are ephemeral, hence some terminologies that refer to this later period as post-urban.[5] Chalcolithic societies

---

[4]B. Allchin and R. Allchin, *The Rise of Civilization in India and Pakistan*, Delhi: Selectbook Service Syndicate, Reprint, 1989, pp. 240, 303.
[5]This period is also often termed as 'Late Harappan'.

after the Mature Harappan are differentiated on the basis of the absence of trademark items such as the distinctive stone weights and the steatite seals. In the Greater Indus Valley, these chalcolithic cultures are Jhukar, Cemetery H, late Siswal and Rangpur IIB-C.[6] These can be largely dated between 1900–1700 BCE, though in some areas the dates may extend to 1500 BCE.

In the Sutlej–Yamuna Divide upto western Uttar Pradesh, from about 1900 to about 1000 BCE, we have numerous small settlements with ceramics ranging from those relating to the chalcolithic cultures mentioned above, to the Ochre Coloured Pottery (OCP).[7] To summarize the information from these small settlements means taking note of a less diverse (as compared to the Harappan) material culture that includes ceramics, a few terracotta artefacts, and a considerable amount of copper-bronze artefacts, as well as a conspicuous lack of architecture made of burnt bricks. In the Ganga–Yamuna Doab are found archaeological deposits called Copper Hoards comprising groups of distinctive copper-bronze objects with almost no trace of habitation. The areas where OCP and Copper Hoards have been found overlap, suggesting a possible correlation between them.

In the early Iron Age, the Painted Grey Ware (PGW) comprises a ceramic found in the region of the Ganga-Yamuna Doab, a ceramic so distinctive that it lends its name to an

---

[6]All these late Harappan cultures are named after sites—Jhukar, Siswal, Rangpur, and Cemetery H after a cemetery at the site of Harappa.
[7]The OCP is named after a type of ceramic found in this region—ochre coloured, porous and with an appearance of being worn out.

archaeological culture. The ceramic has a smooth grey surface with geometric paintings in black. These paintings are found both inside and outside the vessels. This has meant that largely vessels comprise open forms that are used for eating, such as bowls and dishes. This black painted grey ware is also accompanied by iron tools at various sites. However, other than these two features, sites of this period reveal very few artefacts and scarce architecture. Occasionally this ceramic has been preceded by a plain grey ware and sometimes by a black slipped ceramic.

FEATURES OF THE POST-MATURE HARAPPAN PERIOD

The Issue of Regionalization

The aftermath of the Mature Harappan saw the Greater Indus Valley break up into a mosaic of small localized settlements and cultures. The Harappan region saw the Jhukar culture emerge in Sind, Cemetery H in the region of western Punjab[8] and the Cholistan, late Siswal in the Sutlej–Yamuna Divide, and Rangpur IIB-C in Gujarat. Interestingly, in the period before the Mature Harappan too, there had been a roughly similar regionalized pattern. It is in areas outside the urban Harappan region that we see several chalcolithic cultures, some of which began during the Harappan period. Among the chalcolithic cultures, the Sothi–Siswal culture began before the urban Harappan, and continued during and after

---

[8]Western Punjab is in Pakistan, while eastern Punjab comprises present day Punjab and Haryana in India.

its decline, the Ganeshwar–Jodhpura was contemporary to the Mature Harappan while the Ochre Coloured Pottery and the Copper Hoards are found in the aftermath of the Harappan period.

Ceramics have aided in the understanding of regionalization in these periods. In Indian archaeology, pottery often assumes great significance in that 'archaeological cultures' are often distinguished one from another on the basis of ceramics alone. Moreover, while the Harappan period witnessed a largely similar set of ceramics (as envisaged by the term 'culture'), chalcolithic cultures are differentiated through ceramic styles and designs. These ceramic styles are found in smaller geographical enclaves that are exclusive and have been used to suggest a regionalization/localization that can be viewed in material terms. Thus, the Cemetery H ceramics have little in common with the Jhukar or with Rangpur IIB-C. While the later chalcolithic cultures may share a few common features with the preceding Mature Harappan, primary among which is a red-surfaced ceramic with paintings in black, the differences among the ceramics are many and need to be emphasized.

Regarding other artefacts, in the eastern Punjab there seems to be resurgence in the use of faience, an artificially manufactured material, with sites revealing no depletion in the use of this material. This contrasts with other regions, for example, Gujarat, where faience is barely found from Rangpur IIB-C sites. Similarly, round faience seals are found from Jhukar levels, a type of object unknown from the urban Harappan as well as other chalcolithic cultures. Similarly, it is ceramics, with their shapes and designs that have enabled the distinctions between the late Harappan and other chalcolithic cultures, such as OCP, in the Ganga–Yamuna Doab.

At the same time, this aspect of regionalization needs to be seen in contrast with the spread of material traits in the Mature Harappan. It should also be tempered with the evidence of new communities settling particularly on the margins of the erstwhile Mature Harappan region.

Changes in Settlements and Strategies

It is not as if whole societies or communities died out after the urban Harappan, even while areas and settlements were abandoned. Let us take the case of the Cholistan region bordering the Thar Desert in India, where a major survey was undertaken, to show the changes, and ask what kind of settlements are to be found in the post-urban period? The table below gives us a hint:

Figure 1: Types of settlements in the Cholistan Desert over time

Types of sites	Mature Harappan	Cemetery H (late chalcolithic sites)	PGW
Total sites	174	50	14
Industrial/ Production	79	9	0
Settlements with kilns	33	14	0

Settlement sites only	50	14	14
Camp sites	10	13	0
Cemetery sites	2	0	0

(After M. R. Mughal, 1997)

While the categories remain the same across time periods, the interesting difference lies in the number of camp sites as a percentage of the total. In the case of the Cemetery H, this is 26 per cent, as compared to 5.75 per cent in the Mature Harappan period. It does appear that in the later period, there is an increase in the mobile population even if the percentage of settlement sites (with and without kilns) goes up marginally from the Mature Harappan period.

Differences between the Mature Harappan and the later period can be seen in the context of agriculture and other subsistence practices. While people seem to have largely cultivated the same set of crops, we see a greater reliance on rice and summer millets in the later period. There is a suggestion that the Mature Harappans moved towards river systems for irrigation as earlier systems of rain-fed agriculture became more difficult. Interestingly, in the later period, in the Sutlej–Yamuna Divide, there is a reversal of irrigation systems back to rainfall, this time for cultivating summer crops, along with utilizing smaller, more ephemeral rivers. Apart from this, evidence seems to point to crop processing taking place within households in the later period (at least at Harappa and Rojdi in Gujarat) as compared to centralized processing in the urban period. As far as animal husbandry is concerned, too, there seems to be a shift at Harappa from dominance on cattle in the Mature Harappan to sheep and goats, a pattern that was the practice in the chalcolithic levels prior to the Mature Harappan too. From this, Rita P. Wright[9] suggests that animals were less necessary for traction, and for long distance exchange networks. This implies more local, subsistence level communities in the later period. These shifts in animal herding also perhaps suggest a more mobile subsistence strategy in the later period in the Cholistan and Gujarat, where communities may have relied more on agro-pastoralism.

The Issue of Urbanism

Surveys help archaeologists produce settlement distributions of sites that are usually graded into different sizes. Size has often been taken to indicate differences in complexity, and is used to point towards urbanity. It is not surprising that in most time periods, the smallest sites (understood to be villages) outnumber sites of larger sizes. However, with urban decline or the end of the Harappan, there seems to be marked increase in the number of small settlements. Archaeologists also have little doubt that there was a gradual eastward and southward shift in population, away from the Indus Valley. This can account for the proliferation of settlements in Haryana and western Uttar Pradesh to the east and Gujarat towards the south. Where in the Sutlej–Yamuna Divide,

---

[9]Rita P. Wright, *The Ancient Indus*, Cambridge: Cambridge University Press, 2010, p. 322.

for example, a maximum number of 160 Mature Harappan sites can be counted, the number of late Siswal sites in the late 1990s stood at 149 for Haryana and Punjab and 130 for Uttar Pradesh. Madella and Fuller[10] have suggested that crops dependent on summer rainfall, such as millets and rice, produce a lower yield per unit area and may have been less suitable for supporting large urban centres and instead provided sustenance for smaller communities. If we put the latter point together with a general absence of settlements that could be termed as 'urban', we are perhaps seeing the fissioning of the earlier large settlements.

The period from 1900 BCE has usually been considered as one that lay between two urban axes, what are usually called the 'first urbanization' (the Harappan) and the 'second urbanization' (in the Ganga Valley). This interim period has been considered as a period of 'de-urbanization', of regionalization, of ruralization. However, Shaffer and Lichtenstein,[11] have tried to suggest that there was no interregnum or gap in urbanism, that cities continued to exist after 1900 BCE, and that the first and second urbanizations were not separate phenomena but constituted a continuous history of urbanism in the subcontinent. Shaffer used data on certain large (about 40 hectares in size) settlements, to

---

[10]M. Madella and D. Fuller, 'Palaeoecology and the Harappan Civilization of South Asia: A reconsideration', *Quarternary Science Reviews* 25, p. 1298.
[11]J. G. Shaffer and D. A. Lichtenstein, 'Ethnicity and change in the Indus Valley cultural tradition', in J. M. Kenoyer ed., *Old Problems and New Perspectives in the Archaeology of South Asia*, Madison: Wisconsin Archaeological Reports, 1986, pp. 117–26.

show that large-sized sites continued to exist even in the post-urban period. However, size cannot be taken as a sole criterion of urbanism, and only excavation can suggest the presence of urban elements.

Why is urbanism so important? Perhaps this has to do with our modern conceptions of the city, our familiarity with it, and the notion that the city is the most conducive place to live in, with its facilities and services which is reflected in ever-increasing urban migration in contemporary South Asia. The urbanity of the Mature Harappans allows us, in the present, to remember and valorize that urban condition and of being associated in some small way with the old civilizations of Mesopotamia and Egypt. The Harappan Period has always enjoyed a privileged place in Indian archaeology that first began with the concerted efforts to locate Harappan and Harappan-affiliated sites within the borders of India. It can still be seen in more recent proclamations of heightened antiquity and size of the site of Rakhigarhi located in Haryana. To date, information on sites that show urban features as far away as Tamil Nadu[12] are considered to link the so-called 'Vaigai civilization' with the Indus Civilization, showing the continuing aura of the Harappan culture on the archaeology of India. Towards that end, it becomes imperative to negate the idea of societal fluctuations, and to instead suggest that there was a continuous urban trajectory in the past.[13]

---

[12]For example, Keezhadi in Sivaganga District.

[13]To that end, some archaeologists have tried to trace a long history of settlement in the Greater Indus Valley starting from about 7000 BCE. There is no doubt that there has been continuous settlement in the Greater Indus

The Issue of Transitions

We cannot also see the entire archaeological history of the northwestern part of the Indian subcontinent as one bloc; rather we need to view carefully the periods of transition. Are these seamless or were there sharp disjunctures? There has been some debate over the transition between the earlier chalcolithic cultures and the Mature Harappan. The former are distinguished geographically as well as through their ceramics, and are four in number: Amri/Nal, Kot Diji, Sothi/Siswal and Damb Sadaat.[14] Some scholars see the transitional period as one of continuity,[15] while others have noted the vital changes that emerge with the Mature Harappan, most notably standardized objects, such as weights and seals that suggest the working of an authority. Deposits that indicate large scale burning between the earlier chalcolithic and the Mature Harappan also suggest a violent upheaval, rather than a peaceful continuity between the two periods. In the context of the Mature and various later chalcolithic cultures, there were points of continuity in certain features. However,

---

Valley, but clearly not all of these can be called urban. Occupations prior to the Mature Harappan have, in fact, been called pre-urban, as such occupations have failed to reveal the complexity of society and economy that would characterize urban societies.

[14]All these names derive from actual sites, usually where a certain ceramic was first detected.

[15]Features common between the chalcolithic cultures prior to the Mature Harappan and the Mature Harappan are: a basic subsistence base (wheat, barley, sesame, linseed, dates, sheep, goat, and cattle), the use of brick for construction, the cart for transportation, and wheel-made ceramics with some designs similar to the urban period.

while several sites continued to be occupied in the later period, there was disintegration in the ways of living, and an abandonment of several settlements, with people moving into newer areas to the east and southeast.

It is important to see that both transitions (from earlier chalcolithic-Mature Harappan and the Mature Harappan-later chalcolithic) show aspects in common between the respective chalcolithic societies. For one thing, both periods show regionalization/localization through the evidence of separate material assemblages in separate regions. Materially too, early chalcolithic ceramics, such as Sothi–Siswal survive during the Mature Harappan and emerge as dominant ceramics in the late Siswal in the Sutlej–Yamuna Divide. It is as if the Mature Harappan period overrode local ways of life for a brief period. This has been considered by scholars as prevailing local traditions that are gradually subsumed within the Great Tradition of the Mature Harappan, but which re-emerge after the latter's decline. In that context, agricultural strategies show a similar pattern, as noted above, where rain-fed agriculture (for winter cereals) in the early chalcolithic gave way to river irrigation in the Mature Harappan but are revived in the later chalcolithic for watering summer crops. There are other important technological changes: from Jhukar we now begin to find the paddle-and-anvil technique to make round-based vessels, a technique unknown to the Harappans. Today, this technique is predominant in South Asia, where the wheel is used to make ceramics.

The other important point of transition is between the

later chalcolithic period and the PGW, as a shift from the chalcolithic to the Iron Age. The early Iron Age as marked by the PGW is also important as there has been a prevailing view that this period represents the coming of the Aryans, or rather, people speaking archaic Sanskrit, to the subcontinent. The reasons for this conflation rest on the idea that the PGW is an intrusive ceramic that has no link to preceding archaeological occupations and also because of the fact that PGW layers are marked by the presence of iron artefacts that herald the appearance of new materials and technologies in the subcontinent. The problem with this interpretation is that ceramics cannot be equated to communities of people speaking a particular language.

Archaeologically, the PGW is a fine ceramic and its distinct character has enabled scholars to consider it as diagnostic of an entire material assemblage; hence, the labelling of the culture as PGW. At the same time, it is not the only ceramic found at PGW sites. Other ceramics such as Black-and-Red-Ware (BRW), red wares and other grey wares are also found, but the distinctiveness of PGW has allowed it to get precedence over other ceramics. In fact, archaeologists have done a disservice in privileging PGW over other ceramics, and a study of the accompanying wares may have provided a clearer view of continuities and discontinuities of such sites with other occupations.

Why has this ceramic been considered as intrusive? Perhaps the main reason rests on the technology used to produce vessels in this ceramic. PGW is a grey-surfaced ceramic, produced in a reducing kiln, meaning that vessels were fired in a structure or kiln within which there was no oxygen. This could be a closed structure or vessels completely sealed off from air (oxygen) by putting them in boxes or saggers. In contrast, open kilns with air passing through (even if loosely covered with large broken potsherds) are called oxidizing kilns, and resulted in red-surfaced vessels. Late chalcolithic ceramics were primarily of the latter variety, much like ceramics in the Mature Harappan period. Thus, the introduction of PGW implies the introduction of a new firing technology.

Other than firing, PGW vessels were made by techniques markedly different from those used to produce the earlier red wares. Harappan vessels were thick-walled and sturdy and were made entirely on the wheel. PGW ceramics, on the other hand, were produced through a multi-stage process where the initial throwing was on the wheel. After a partial drying, the vessel was put back on the wheel and vessel walls subsequently thinned by using a sharp tool to trim off excess clay. Styles of painting too differed between the chalcolithic and PGW. The latter used multiple brushes to produce concentric and geometric designs unlike earlier paintings that involved motifs from nature using a single brush technique.

The transition from the chalcolithic to PGW has become a fraught topic in the context of a period considered by some to mark the advent of new communities into the northern part of the subcontinent. In terms of location, PGW sites are found from Cholistan and the Sutlej-Yamuna Divide eastwards to the Ganga–Yamuna Doab. Thus, following other post-urban cultures, this ceramic is found at sites on the eastern margins of the Greater Indus Valley. Many sites after the Mature Harappan have either been identified as chalcolithic or PGW. In the Cholistan, not a single chalcolithic site reveals PGW ceramics, suggesting the occupation of new areas. From the Sutlej–Yamuna Divide eastwards to the Ganga, too, many small chalcolithic sites were abandoned, and the distribution of PGW sites suggest a discontinuity between the former (both Late Siswal and Cemetery H) and PGW occupations. However, excavations at one site, Bhagwanpura in Kurukshetra District of Haryana, have revealed a transitional phase between chalcolithic and PGW suggesting continuity between these two periods at this site.[16] This comprises important information and needs to be corroborated from other sites. Moreover, what does this transition mean? The excavator of Bhagwanpura[17] suggests that people who used chalcolithic ceramics and PGW belonged to different communities who mingled together at the settlement. He even notes the use of both ceramics within the same house at Bhagwanpura. It is these finds and their contexts that need to be better understood in order to understand a transition.

---

[16]At Dadheri, Katpalon and Nagar, too, continuity between chalcolithic and PGW has been noted.

[17]J. P. Joshi, *Excavation at Bhagwanpura 1975-76 and other Explorations & Excavations 1975-1981 in Haryana, Jammu & Kashmir and Punjab*, New Delhi: Archaeological Survey of India, 1993, pp. 18–19.

ARCHAEOLOGY AND THE ARYAN QUESTION

Why is the issue of continuity so significant? For some, the Aryans or Sanskrit-speaking people never came from outside; instead, Sanskrit speakers moved from their subcontinental homeland westwards. Much of the debate over the origin of the Aryans rests on linguistic data, but since our concern is archaeological, the following threads become relevant: (i) the claim for biological continuity; (ii) settlement patterns along the Ghaggar/Hakra and; (iii) the presence/absence of the horse. Regarding the last, until now a few animal bones at one or two Harappan sites have been identified as belonging to the *Equus* family. There is, however, no consensus between archaeozoologists differing over the species of *Equus* found at Harappan sites: *Equus hemionus* (the Asiatic half-ass) or *Equus caballus* (the 'true' horse).

The number and distribution of Harappan sites in Pakistan was to alter drastically with the surveys conducted from 1974 by M. Rafique Mughal, a leading Pakistani archaeologist. His survey in the Cholistan Desert gave new data on 174 Mature Harappan sites along the Hakra. Since this became the largest concentration of Harappan sites, the Cholistan was proclaimed as the nuclear area of the Indus Civilization. This became a cause of debate with certain archaeologists preferring to identify the Ghaggar/Hakra with the Sarasvati, the major river of the *Rig Veda*. However, while the number of sites is large, most are very small in size. At the same time, we should remember that it is far easier for archaeologists to survey along a dry river bed than along an active one like the Indus or any of the Punjab rivers.

As far as biological data is concerned, a study of skeletal data in the early 1990s[18] suggested that there was no evidence of the incursion of a new population into the subcontinent in the period after Harappan decline. Instead, two discontinuities, one between 6000 and 4500 BCE, and the other between 800 and 200 BCE have been suggested based on dental and craniometric evidence. The cranial data has been suggested to reveal interactions with the west, more specifically with the Iranian Plateau. However, this debate was prior to recent studies on ancient DNA.

The Genetic Picture

Archaeology has provided important data comprising skeletons with the potential of contributing ancient DNA. However, even though a few Harappan and later chalcolithic sites have revealed cemeteries, little attempt was made to recover DNA, either because techniques had not yet been developed for older excavations, or because the samples were poor. A Harvard study led by David Reich has suggested, on the basis of modern DNA, that the people of India today are the outcome of mixtures between two highly differentiated populations: 'Ancestral North Indians' (ANI) and 'Ancestral South Indians' (ASI).[19] The study has suggested that there

---

[18]Brian E. Hemphill, John R. Lukacs, and K.A.R. Kennedy, Biological adaptations and affinities of Bronze Age Harappans, in Richard H. Meadow, ed., *Harappa Excavations 1986-1990*, Madison: Prehistory Press, 1991, pp. 137–82.

[19]David Reich, *Who We Are and How We Got Here*, New York: Pantheon Books, 2018.

were two major migrations that have resulted in the population mix that can be seen at present in the subcontinent. The first was that of farmers migrating into India from the core region of the Near East or Iran after 9,000 years ago who interbred with the previously established hunter-gatherer populations to form new mixed groups that can be called the ASI. This mix comprised 25 per cent Iranian farmers and 75 per cent previously established hunter-gatherers of South Asia. The second migration began from Central Asia about 5,000 years ago and the effects can be dated to about 4,000–3,500 years ago within South Asia, in other words, to just about after the Harappan decline. This migration resulted in the ANI, a mixture of about 50 per cent steppe ancestry related distantly to the Yamnaya, and about 50 per cent Iranian farmer-related ancestry from the groups the steppe people encountered as they expanded south. Reich,[20] incidentally, also suggested that the Yamnaya are obvious candidates for spreading Indo–European languages to the Indian subcontinent.

Reich's study did not have access to ancient DNA from the subcontinent. He does suggest three possibilities regarding the Indus Valley people: (i) they were largely unmixed descendants of the first Iranian-related farmers of the region, and spoke an early Dravidian language; (ii) they were the ASI, already a mix of people related to Iranian farmers and South Asian hunter-gatherers, and if so, would also have spoken a Dravidian language, and (iii) they were the ANI, already mixed between steppe and Iranian farmer-related ancestry,

---

[20]Reich, *Who We Are*, p. 152.

and thus would instead likely have spoken an Indo–European language.

Thus, the issue of obtaining ancient DNA assumes urgency, and in this context, the skeletons from Rakhigarhi and the extraction of DNA from them are crucial.

While the data has not yet been published, news reports indicate that Rakhigarhi samples were analysed by Niraj Rai of Birbal Sahni Institute in Lucknow's Ancient DNA Lab. A paper co-authored with Harvard geneticist Vageesh Narasimhan et al., whose publication is imminent suggests that the Harappans had Ancestral South Indian (ASI) genes with no Central Asian genetic mix.

CULTURES IN CONTACT

As far as language is concerned, it must be reiterated that the advent of Old Indo–Aryan or Sanskrit into South Asia is an issue to be dealt with by linguists, not by archaeologists. At most, if the Harappan seals had been deciphered, they may have provided a clue to the language(s) that the Harappans spoke. Similarly, while skeletons can be recovered archaeologically, it is futile to link them with speakers of a particular language. An equally futile tendency has been to try and associate a language (in this case, Sanskrit) and speakers of that language with archaeological material, such as the PGW.

At the same time, archaeological evidence does point to cultures in contact over the millennia. It seems that the demise of the Harappan culture led to a vacuum that was filled in various ways. While communities continued to occupy some of the older settlements, many moved away to newer areas, and other communities and peoples came in to fill the gaps, with new ways of living and new technologies, such as reducing kilns, more efficient transportation, and the hafting of metal tools. This is, thus, a period that sees an influx of people from the west and northwest, as can be seen by the cemeteries in Baluchistan and Gandhara. Similarly, material from the oasis settlements of Bactria and Margiana [the Bactria–Margiana Archaeological Culture (BMAC)] have been found in the Jhukar levels at Mohenjodaro and Chanhudaro, as well as from late levels at Harappa. Gregory Possehl makes it a point to write: 'There is no reason to believe that any of the peoples of the BMAC or their predecessors were speakers of an Indo–European language, let along Vedic Sanskrit. There is a possibility that some of these peoples spoke a language or languages of this family, but a closely reasoned case let alone proof for this has never been offered.'[21] It is interesting that when we get into the period after the Mature Harappan, there seems to be a need to examine and judge whether any archaeological material that appears intrusive to the subcontinent and originating from the north and northwest can be related to the Aryans. Perhaps it would be better to see this period as similar to preceding ones where despite local and regional ties, there would have been interactions with and movements of people from other areas. Thus, we may also be able to explain the recent finds at Sanauli in Baghpat District of Uttar Pradesh.

---

[21]G. L. Possehl, *The Indus Civilization: A Contemporary Perspective*, New Delhi: Vistaar, 2002, p. 232.

The cemetery at Sanauli has been labelled by its excavators, in 2004, as 'late Harappan' on the basis of its ceramics, and is significant for various reasons. For one, it is fairly large with 116 burials having been excavated and its full extent still unknown; second, there are 29 symbolic burials where there is no skeleton but in all other senses appears to be similar to the burial format of the others; third, several burials are notable for unique features: two have antennae-swords within the burials; two have a thin plate of a rough figure-of-eight design on which one had copper elements decorating the edge while the other had rows of steatite inlays along the edge; two burials have glass beads among grave goods; and there are gold objects found within other burials, as also ceramics, beads, and animal remains as part of burial goods, suggesting at least some high status burials, in contrast to the uniformity of the Mature Harappan burials.[22] Recently, in 2018, the site was excavated again and a burial has been found associated with a chariot with solid wooden wheels covered with copper, along with coffins with copper decorations in the form of anthropomorphic figures. The finds of antennae-swords from Sanauli within burials has given a context for objects that so far have been found within Copper Hoards, and only occasionally associated with OCP. The find of the chariot at Sanauli assumes significance if we

---

[22]See D. V. Sharma, K. C. Nauriyal, V. N. Prabhakar and Vishnukant, 'Sanauli: A late Harappan burial site in the Yamuna-Hindon Doab', *Puratattva* 34: 35-44, 2003–04; D. V. Sharma, K. C. Nauriyal and V. N. Prabhakar, Excavations at Sanauli 2005–06: A Harappan necropolis in the Upper Ganga-Yamuna Doab, *Puratattva* 36:, 2005–06, pp. 166–79.

consider the suggestion[23] of small raiding groups using horse-drawn chariots moving southeastwards from the Iranian region towards the Indian subcontinent.

Sanauli is an important site as it contextualizes some of the materials that are pieces within a larger mosaic of chalcolithic cultures that are evident in the aftermath of the Mature Harappan. The evidence needs to be studied carefully as the site was damaged by farmers prior to excavation, and the finds of glass beads in a chalcolithic context may suggest contamination. Perhaps it is also time we consider the site and its finds as a distinct entity, separate from any Harappan influence, especially in the context of the stark differences with Mature Harappan cemeteries. Sanauli is also important as it shows us the potential of the area east of the Indus valley in providing a hint of the movement of people in a highly significant period. While most history books will gloss over this period, between 2000 and 500 BCE, preferring to focus on the urban Harappans, what we note is a period vital for settling new regions, developing diverse livelihood strategies and bringing in new technologies. This period also enables a necessary decentring of the focus from the large cities with their long-ranging networks to the small, the mobile, and the local, and also remind us that there were small settlements with local networks in the Mature Harappan too that have long been neglected.

---

[23]S. Ratnagar, *The Aryan homeland debate in India*, in P. L. Kohl, M. Kozelsky and N. Ben-Yehuda, eds., *Selective Remembrances: Archaeology in the Construction, Commemoration, and Consecration of National Pasts*, Chicago and London: Chicago University press, 2007, p. 361–62.

THE COMPLICATIONS OF GENETICS

KAI FRIESE

The 'petrous bone' is an inelegant but useful chunk of the human skull—basically it protects your inner ear. But that's not all it protects. In recent years, genetic scientists working to extract DNA from ancient skeletons have discovered that thanks to the extreme density of a particular region of the petrous bone (the bit shielding the cochlea), they could sometimes harvest a hundred times more DNA from it than from any other tissue in human remains.

Now this somewhat macabre innovation may well resolve one of the most heated debates about the history of India. When the dust of the petrous bones of a 4,500-year-old skeleton from Rakhigarhi, Haryana, settles, we should have the answer to a few questions that have vexed some of the best minds in history and science—and a lot of mediocre politicians along the way:

Q: Were the people of the Harappan civilization the original source of the Sanskritic language and culture of Vedic Hinduism?
A: No.

Q: Do their genes survive as a significant component in India's current population?

119

A: Most definitely.

Q: Were they closer to popular perceptions of 'Aryans' or of 'Dravidians'?
A: Dravidians.

Q: Were they more akin to the South Indians or North Indians of today?
A: South Indians.

All loaded questions. But a much-anticipated research paper suggesting these conclusions is likely to be accessible online within months. Drafts of the paper have already been circulated to researchers and interested journalists including this writer.

These revelations are part of the long awaited and much-postponed results of an excavation conducted in 2015 by a team led by Dr Vasant Shinde, an archaeologist and vice chancellor of Pune's Deccan College. Why did it take so long? One answer was on offer a year ago when this writer spoke to Shinde who was then holding out the promise of publishing the findings in September 2017: 'It's a very politically sensitive issue,' he said. The archaeologist may have been referring to the fact that any research dealing with the Harappan civilization would have to confront the Hindutva agenda of the BJP government at the Centre—whose politics demands a genuflection to Vedic Hinduism as the origin of Indian civilization. For historians or anyone working on the Harappan or Indus Valley Civilization (IVC) this is a complication. Indeed, when the IVC was first 'discovered' in the 1920s colonial archaeologists quickly identified it as evidence of a pre-Vedic culture, which, they theorized, had been utterly destroyed by the advent of 'Aryan' invaders from the Northwest who represented the dawn of Hindu India.

In later years most mainstream historians have discarded the 'Aryan Invasion theory' or 'AIT' as an oversimplification—while retaining a chronology that places the Vedic civilization as *a successor* to the IVC. And the AIT continues to rankle Hindutva nationalists even as it has taken root in South India as the core narrative of a popular politics which sees the IVC as a Dravidian culture that has survived 'Brahminical' invaders only south of the Vindhyas.

GREAT EXPECTATIONS

Meanwhile, the reality of who the IVC people were has remained a mystery. Dr Shinde knows all too well the incongruous burden of expectations that have now settled on a 4,500 year old resident (classified as 'I4411') of Rakhigarhi, a ramshackle village in the dusty khadar or floodplain of an almost extinguished river. Over the last decade and a half Rakhigarhi has become a staple of school textbooks, tourism pamphlets and journalism—invoked as the largest Harappan/Indus Valley site in India. In fact, since 2014 it has been regularly cited as 'even larger than Mohenjodaro'—the legendary archaeological site in Sindh, Pakistan, first excavated in the 1920s.

Despite the element of hyperbole, excavations here which have been conducted intermittently since the late 1960s have established its significance as an extensive and enduring urban settlement with its beginnings arguably as early as the seventh millennium BCE. Most importantly, the village with its seven teelas or mounds has produced enough evidence to identify it as the site of a 'mature' Harappan settlement of the second and third millennium BCE. In other words, a town that witnessed the rise and—more than four thousand years ago—the mysterious fall, of India's first urban civilization.

On the face of it, the single most startling revelation of the Rakhigarhi research may be what it doesn't talk about: the complete absence of any reference to the genetic marker[1] R1a1 in the ancient DNA retrieved from the site. This is significant because R1a1, often loosely called 'the 'Aryan gene', is now understood to have originated in a population of bronze age pastoralists who dispersed from a homeland in the 'Pontic steppe' (the grasslands sprawling between the Black Sea and the Caspian, abutting Central Asia) some four thousand years ago. The genetic impact of their migrations has left a particularly strong and 'sex-biased', (i.e. male-driven) imprint on the populations of two geographically distant but linguistically related parts of the world: Northern India and Northern Europe. 'We are not discussing R1a,' said Niraj Rai, the lead genetic researcher on the Rakhigarhi DNA project. 'R1a is not there.' The admission came wrapped in some prevarication but was all the more telling given that the

---

[1]R1a, also classified as R-M420, is a haplogroup of human Y-chromosome DNA thought to have emerged in Eurasia more than 20,000 years ago. Its subclade R1a1a diversified some 6,000 years ago to spawn the lineages R1a-Z282 (associated with North European populations), and R1a-Z93 (associated more strongly with Asian populations).

Rakhigarhi data presented in this paper are derived primarily from the genetic material of 'I4411', a male individual—R1a is a mutation seen only in samples of the male Y chromosome.

The absence of this genetic imprint in the first DNA sample of an individual from the Indus Valley Culture will bolster what is already a consensus among genetic scientists, historians and philologists–that the Indus Valley Culture preceded and was distinct from this population of cattle-herding, horse-rearing, chariot-driving, battle-axe-wielding, proto-Sanskrit-speaking migrants whose ancestry is most evident in high-caste North Indian communities today. Rai did point out that the fact that R1a did not show up in the Rakhigarhi sample could be attributed to the limited amount of genetic data retrieved. Or it could be because it's just not there. 'We do not have much coverage of the Y chromosome regions [of the genome],' Rai said revealing that they had retrieved more data from the mitochondrial and autosomal DNA in their sample (mitochondrial DNA reflects maternal descent and autosomal tests reveal genetic information inherited from both parents). However, he was emphatic in acknowledging that while 'a mass movement of Central Asians happened and significantly changed the South Asian genetic makeup', the inhabitants of ancient Rakhigarhi 'do not have any affinity with the Central Asians'. In other words, while the citizens of the Indus Valley Civilization had none of this ancestry, you, dear average Indian reader, owe some 17.5 per cent of your male lineage to people from the steppe. It's worth noting that this genetic footprint is of an entirely more impressive order than the relatively inconsequential biological legacy of more recent Islamic or European colonial invasions that often preoccupy the political imagination in India.

So much for what we have now learned about who our 4,500-year-old ancestor 'I4411' was not. What about who he was? The short answer according to Rai is that I4411 'has more affinity with South Indian tribal populations'. Notably the Irula in the Nilgiri highlands. Indeed a draft of the Rakhigarhi paper suggests that this individual could be modelled as being a clade [a group sharing descent from a common ancestor] with Irula...but not with groups with higher proportions of West Eurasian related ancestry such as Punjabis and goes on to suggest that the inhabitants of Rakhigarhi probably spoke an early Dravidian language. However, the results also show clear evidence of mixing with another population from outside the subcontinent labelled 'Iranian agriculturalist'. This is a population that had been identified in earlier studies of ancient DNA and is consistent with the hypothesis that some agricultural technologies were introduced to the subcontinent through contact with the 'fertile crescent', in West Asia, widely regarded as one of the birthplaces of Eurasian agriculture in the fifth to eighth millennium BCE.

For an older generation of Indians the Rakhigarhi results may sound like a reboot of half-remembered schoolbooks: 'Dravidian' Harappans followed by Vedic Horsemen from the steppe. And for anyone who has been following more recent developments in population genetics, too, the latest findings will sound familiar. Meanwhile, in the popular press, coverage of recent discoveries in the archaeology or genetics of Harappan India has been obsessively and distractingly focussed on the 'Aryan Invasion Theory'. What gives? And why does it matter? The answer has to do with the fact that recent years have been a very busy time in ancient Indian history. And modern Indian politics.

SKULDUGGERY

In the months preceding the news of the Rakhigarhi findings, anticipation was high, and fuelled by a series of related research papers and their journalistic glosses, an acrimonious, if occasionally amusing, debate erupted on social media. Professor Shinde for his part was given to dropping broad hints that the Rakhigarhi results would point to a 'continuity' between the population of the ancient town and its present day inhabitants (predominantly Jats, a population marked by pronounced R1a steppe ancestry).

Perhaps it should be no surprise, in these fractious times, that fake news would be deployed as a weapon in the civil war that has consumed ancient Indian history. *Dainik Jagran* carried an article[2] purportedly based on an interview with Niraj Rai, asserting that the Rakhigarhi DNA was in fact a close match for North Indian Brahmins and that the findings would establish that India was the 'native place' of the Indo–European language family.

'Utter Crud!' was the reaction of David Wesolowski, host

---

[2] 4 January 2018, https://www.jagran.com/news/national-jagran-special-on-indo-european-languages-17304852.html

of the Eurogenes blog—well regarded by some of the world's leading geneticists as a go-to site for the latest gossip and fierce debate. Wesolowski's site witnessed frequent arguments over the likelihood that Rakhigarhi DNA would turn up the R1a1 marker. Here, extended and nuanced discussions of the finer points of molecular evidence would often conclude with kiss-offs along the lines of 'you're an idiot' or 'you're going to need psychiatric help when the results are out'. In the event, Wesolowski's own prediction, 'Expect no R1a in Harappa but a lot of ASI [Ancestral South Indians],' would prove to be spot on.

Behind the surly invective and the journalistic misdirection were rumours and whispers of a face-off between a rising tide of scientific evidence and the political pressures of nativist, Hindutva sentiments in India. The saga of 'Hindutvist history' is by now another familiar tale, with its origins in early Hindu nationalist reaction to colonial archaeology and linguistics, a dogged obsession with refuting the 'Aryan Invasion theory'. It is perhaps most clearly expressed in an irate passage from former RSS Sarsangchalak M. S. Golwalkar's memoir *Bunch of Thoughts*[3]

> It was the wily foreigner, the Britisher, who...carried on the insidious propaganda that we were never one nation, that we were never the children of the soil but mere upstarts having no better claim than the foreign hordes of Muslims or the British over this country.

[3]M. S. Golwalkar, *Bunch of Thoughts*, Bangalore: Vikrama Prakashan, 1966, p. 81.

In recent years, this resentful impulse has focussed particularly intently on asserting the wishful conclusion that the Indus Valley Civilization itself must be 'Vedic'. This has understandably gained traction in the popular imagination in tandem with the political rise of Hindutva. In 2013, Amish Tripathi, a bestselling author of 'Hinduistical fantasy' novels gave vent to the keening desire for a 'Vedic IVC' in a short fiction in which future archaeologists discover clinching evidence 'that the Indus Valley civilisation and the Vedic-erroneously called Aryan-civilisation were one and the same'. The story is poignantly titled 'Science Validates Vedic History'[4].

Inevitably, the advent of a BJP majority government in the general elections of 2014 has given new energy—and funding—to the self-gratifying urges of Hindutvist history. The charge has been led by the Minister of Culture Mahesh Sharma, who has prioritized the project of 'rewriting Indian History' whether by appointing a pliant obscurantist as head of a venerable institution funding historical research or promoting the 'research' of para-scientific outfits such as I-SERVE (Institute of Scientific Research on Vedas) and a former customs officer who uses hobby astronomy software to establish that 'Thus Shri Ram was born on 10th January in 5114 BC around 12 to 1 noontime' [in Ayodhya]. In March 2018, a Reuters report[5] revealed details of a meeting of a

---

[4] Amish Tripathi, 'Science Validates Vedic History', *India Today*, 30 November 2013.

[5] Rupam Jain, Tom Lasseter, 'Special Report: By rewriting history, Hindu nationalists aim to assert their dominance over India', *Reuters*, 6 March 2018.

'History Committee' convened by Mahesh Sharma at the office of the Director General of the Archaeological Survey of India (ASI) in January 2017. Its task, according to the committee chairman K. N. Dixit, was 'to present a report that will help the government rewrite certain aspects of ancient history'. The minutes of the meeting apparently 'set out its aims: to use evidence such as archaeological finds and DNA to prove that today's Hindus are directly descended from the land's first inhabitants many thousands of years ago, and make the case that ancient Hindu scriptures are fact, not myth.'

Yet, if the 'rewriting of Indian History' was lurching ahead on the Hindutva fringe of academia, mainstream science was steadily advancing in quite another direction. In March 2018, the Harvard population geneticist David Reich published an overview of the state of research in his field, the surprise bestseller *Who We Are And How We Got Here*, including an account of how the extreme sensitivity of leading Indian scientists about earlier evidence suggesting an ancient migration of Eurasian people from the Northwest into the subcontinent had nearly scuppered an important scientific collaboration in 2008. The Indian scientists Lalji Singh and K. Thangaraj 'implied that the suggestion of a migration... would be politically explosive,' Reich writes. The issue was ultimately resolved by means of a terminological sleight-of-hand—using the nomenclature 'Ancestral South Indians' (ASI) and 'Ancestral North Indians' (ANI) to obscure the revelation that ANI represented a population with a significant genetic contribution from outside the subcontinent. But the same dynamic appears to have emerged later around a paper involving both Reich and his team at Harvard on the one hand and the scientists leading the Rakhigarhi project on the other. Entitled, rather flatly, 'The Genomic Formation of South and Central Asia' this paper (usually referred to by the shorthand 'M. Narasimhan et al.')—made public as a 'pre-print' in April 2018—would make headlines in the Indian press and social media and reveal some more of the political pressures that colour research on ancient Indian history today. Shinde informed this writer that he had complained to Reich about an earlier draft of that paper, and insisted that any reference to 'migrations' into South Asia be avoided. Or else. He suggested the more ambivalent term 'interaction' be used instead. Given that Shinde controlled access to the Rakhigarhi samples which Reich was keen to work on, this would have been a potent threat, and indeed Narasimhan et al. manages to eschew the term 'migration' entirely while ultimately making more potent statements about the impact of post-Harappan 'Middle to Late Bronze Age' (MLBA) steppe populations on the Indian gene pool. However, the timing of the paper remains curious to say the least, given that it would clearly have benefitted from the Rakhigarhi data which it seemed to pre-empt—despite the fact that several of its co-authors, including Rai, Shinde, Thangaraj, Narasimhan and Reich now share credit for the mysteriously delayed Rakhigarhi paper.

The official word on this was that the Rakhigarhi research was behind schedule due to the 'contamination of one sample' but at the time the geneticist community was abuzz with rumours that the slowdown was because of the Indian team's discomfort with politically inconvenient results. According to one US-based researcher who prefers to remain anonymous, 'It was common knowledge through the grapevine that the Harvard team became impatient and eventually pushed to release their pre-print before Indian colleagues were totally comfortable. Some samples [read 'Rakhigarhi'] were removed because of disagreements between collaborators.'

In more recent conversations with this writer, Professor Shinde seemed intent on dissembling the results of his own team's paper, offering that the results showed that Rakhigarhi's ancient inhabitants were 'just like the locals [of today]...with some contact with South Indian Tribals'. More peculiarly, in a recent interview with *Outlook* magazine, Shinde suggests that the ancient people of Rakhigarhi were 'tall and sharp-featured like the modern Haryanvis.'

However, Professor Shinde is no geneticist, and from what we now know, the Rakhigarhi study essentially endorses the findings of Narasimhan et al.—indeed it can be seen as a companion piece to that earlier work of common authors. Significantly, while Narasimhan et al., predicted a model of the Harappan genome using samples of DNA from ancient skeletons of apparent Indus Valley 'visitors' found in sites that were in trading contact with the Harappans, as well as remains of post-Harappan (1200 BCE–1 CE) individuals from Swat Valley, the Rakhigarhi paper suggests that this model was accurate. The draft recommends that the Narasimhan paper's tentative label of 'Indus Valley Periphery' for this model is a significant match for citizen I4411 of Rakhigarhi and that this genetic cluster should now be recognized as the 'Harappan Cline'.

IT'S STILL COMPLICATED

As the results of the Rakhigarhi study leak steadily into the public domain, a political backlash seems inevitable—and largely predictable—some exultation from Dravidianists and the legion of anti-Hindutva Indians for many of whom the fall of Delhi in the 2014 election is often seen as a replay of that fabled 'Vedic Aryan Invasion'. And we can certainly expect sullen scepticism from the saffron right. Intriguingly, some of the strongest reservations about the Rakhigarhi project have already been expressed from an unexpected quarter: Romila Thapar, an authority on ancient Indian history and a perennial target of Hindutva polemic, has followed the genetics story keenly but expressed some reservations about this new science, particularly with regard to issues of 'contamination', sample size, and the problems of investigating new sources of information. As it turns out this was in fact an initial problem with the Rakhigarhi research—and apparently a misleading 'East Asian' signal in the early data is the reason why the Korean scientists who first worked on the samples have not been credited in the final paper. Meanwhile, historian and archaeologist, Nayanjot Lahiri, declared complete disinterest in the work on 'Harappan DNA', voicing impatience at the obsession with the 'Aryan' question and scepticism about the narrow sampling of ancient genetic material. 'In any case as far as the whole question of Aryans and the Vedic component in Indus Civilization etc., goes—until the Harappan script is deciphered it's not decided,' she said.

While such responses may be unduly harsh—even small genetic samples can reveal considerable demographic depth and geneticists are in any case expanding the range of samples at an impressive rate—some cold water is not amiss. Certainly any triumphalism or despair on the basis of the emerging genetic profile of the 'Harappan Indians' would be misplaced. While the evidence does point convincingly to the IVC being a distinct population from the 'post-Vedic' population infused with MLBA steppe genes that stamp India's population to this day, it's also the case that the IVC population represents 'the single most important source of ancestry in South Asia' today (as Narasimhan et al. puts it). Similarly, any impulse to equate the apparent Dravidian affinities of ancient IVC people with the culture and people of South India today or to cast the latter as the 'original inhabitants' of the subcontinent would be a wild exaggeration. Quite apart from the fact that the people and cultures across the subcontinent today display evidence of having mixed with each other (and populations beyond the borders of present day India) over millennia, there is also no population in the region that can claim to represent a 'pure' lineage of ancient Indians. Not even the Irula or any other South Indian or 'Adivasi' group. Nor should the evidence of the deeply intertwined genetic history of Indian communities lull anyone into a cosy fable of Indic cosmopolitanism. What our DNA tells us instead is that while India did witness phases of extensive genetic mixing for nearly a millennium after the collapse of the IVC, this was followed by a long period of deep endogamy—which has been a uniquely unhealthy stamp of the subcontinent. David Reich summed it up sharply in his book:

> People tend to think of India, with its more than 1.3 billion people, as having a tremendously large population...But genetically, this is an incorrect way to view the situation. The Han Chinese are truly a large population. They have been mixing freely for thousands of years...The truth is that India is composed of a large number of small populations.[6]

If this sounds complicated, that's because it is. And the more we discover about India's past, the more complicated it is likely to become. One of the more intriguing asides in the Rakhigarhi study, is a suggestion that while the IVC population was evidently multi-ethnic, a persistent genetic 'substructure' also indicates that the Harappan civilization may have been characterized by 'high within-group endogamy'.

Such teasers indicate that there is still much work to be done, of course, but they are also reminders not to jump to conclusions or project modern fantasies onto an ancient civilization we still know so little about. And in truth this has been a pathology of the 'liberal' imagination in India as much as it has been of the 'Hindutvist.' In that foundational text of Indian nationalism, *The Discovery of India*, Jawaharlal

---

[6]David Reich, *Who We Are and How We Got Here: Ancient DNA and the New science of the Human Past.* London: Oxford University Press, 2018.

Nehru himself could not resist a moment of secularist rapture when he first set eyes on the ruins of Mohenjodaro: 'What was the secret of this strength? Where did it come from?' he wondered. 'It was, surprisingly enough, a predominantly secular civilisation, and the religious element, though present, did not dominate the scene.'

At the end of the day, 'Chacha' Nehru's vision too is a modern nationalist fantasy, of a piece with the familiar type of the 'Everything comes from India' Uncle. In the years to come we are certain to discover much more about the enduringly mysterious civilization of the Harappans and what elements of culture and social behaviour they bequeathed us—along with their genes. For now, miraculously, their *ears* are speaking. We would do well to listen for a while.

GENETIC ORIGINS OF INDO-ARYANS

RAZIB KHAN

History books have traditionally rested upon the painstaking decryption of ancient texts. The record of prehistory in turn has been gleaned from the unearthing of lost cities and discarded potsherds. Today, genetics is prising apart previously hidden pages of the book of life, allowing scholars to gaze deep into the past and trace migrations hidden even from myth and legend.

DNA is often analogized to a blueprint. But the evolutionary biologist Richard Dawkins maintains a far stronger analogue is a recipe.[1] There is no one-to-one-correspondence between you and your genome. There is no 'gene for your eyes', but rather a complex set of genetic instructions which operate in concert to allow for the unfolding of the developmental process which ultimately yields the various tissues which combine to create the 'eye'.

Variation in these genes explains how some humans have black skin and others white, or why some populations are short and others tall. But the portions of the human genome that code for proteins are only about 1 per cent

---

[1] Richard Dawkins, *The Blind Watchmaker*, New York: Norton, 1986.

of the total sequence length of three billion base pairs.[2] To date, researchers have not reached a consensus over why 99 per cent of the human genome does not consist of 'genes' as classically understood.

Instead, they have found uses for these vast regions of DNA as a 'tracer' for genealogy. The variation across much of the human genome is likely 'neutral' to the direct force of natural selection, where a region of the genome has a fitness effect. This means that as variants drift in and out of the genome over time, researchers can create a model assigning observed variation to processes such as mutation, drift, and gene flow. They can use patterns in the genome to establish relationships between individuals and populations.

To be concrete, a gene involved in a critical biochemical pathway is unlikely to have much variation across humanity. Whether one is Asian, African, or European, this gene will have much the same sequence. Mutations in such genes are likely to be harmful.

Now consider a sequence of the genome which does not code for a functional gene. Negative selection cannot be counted upon to cull such new mutations from the genome, as they pass from parent to child and proliferate across related pedigrees. Instead, the variation will accumulate and family lines will progressively diverge, with particular lineages marked out as genetically distinct. The more distantly two

---

[2]Ng, S. B., Turner, E. H., Robertson, P. D., Flygare, S. D., Bigham, A. W., Lee, C., & Bamshad, M., Targeted capture and massively parallel sequencing of 12 human exomes. *Nature*, 461(7261), 2009, p. 272.

individuals are related the more likely they are to have very different accumulated mutations or genetic variants. Those variants where the new mutation occurs in high numbers within a given population are often termed 'polymorphisms', and those genomic positions are 'polymorphic sites'.

There are on the order of 100 million polymorphisms in human populations, with the typical individual human genome displaying about five million differences from the standard human genome, as defined by the Human Genome Project.[3] That is a great deal of variation to work with in making inferences about the human past. Just twenty years ago researchers could rely upon only a thousand or so genes when drawing inferences.[4]

In the last decades of the twentieth century much of historical genetic inference relied on mitochondrial DNA (mtDNA).[5] There are three primary reasons for this. First, mtDNA is copious, so easier to extract than nuclear DNA. Second, there is a part of the mtDNA genome which was observed to be highly mutable, the 'hypervariable region' (HVR). This provides a great deal of variation for researchers to utilize in their analyses. And third, mtDNA passes down the generations only from mother to daughter (although sons inherit their mother's mtDNA, they are 'dead ends',

---

[3] 1000 Genomes Project Consortium, 'A global reference for human genetic variation'. *Nature*, *526*(7571), 2015, p. 68.

[4] Luigi Luca Cavalli-Sforza, Paolo Menozzi, Alberto Piazza, *The History and Geography of Human Genes*, Princeton: Princeton University Press, 1994.

[5] R. L. Cann, M. Stoneking & A. C. Wilson, 'Mitochondrial DNA and Human Evolution', *Nature*, *325*(6099), 1987, pp. 31-36.

unable to pass it to their offspring). While most of the human genome 'recombines', so that we inherit complex palimpsests assembled together from numerous ancestors, mtDNA satisfies a phylogenetic tree. This means that even modest computers could analyse the data and make inferences.

Phylogenetic methods which relied on late twentieth-century computational capacity were amenable to tree-like representations, rather than the more complex pedigrees which are the norm in within-species analyses, where many ancestors may occupy multiple positions in the tree. The utilization of mtDNA, and later the Y chromosome, which like mtDNA travels down a single lineage (from father to son), did allow for broad generalizations to be made which have mostly held true. Just as with mtDNA, Y-chromosomal phylogenetic trees implied that Africa was the ancestral home of all modern humans.[6] Human populations outside of Africa held far less genetic diversity as a whole than human populations within Africa. The branches of the human family outside of Africa for both the mtDNA and Y chromosome were nested within the broader African range of genetic variation.

Historically, if non-Africans are descended from a small branch of Africans, then they will have had only a small proportion of the genetic variation of ancestral humans. Non-Africans will accumulate new genetic mutations distinct to

---

[6] P. A. Underhill, P. Shen, A. A. Lin, L. Jin, G. Passarino, W. H. Yang & M. Ibrahim, 'Y chromosome sequence variation and the history of human populations', *Nature genetics*, 26 (3), 2000, p. 358.

their lineage, but if their expansion was recent, time wouldn't yet have been sufficient to replenish their diversity via mutation. The two major findings from this period of research were that non-Africans went through a major population bottleneck recently, ergo their reduced diversity, and that they seem to be well modelled as a subset of the diverse African populations.

Since 2000, the discoveries in the field of human population-genetic inference and phylogenetics have shifted away from mtDNA and Y chromosomes, expanding to whole-genome analyses. Using hundreds of thousands of markers, researchers have been able to construct much more robust patterns of relationships of modern populations. As noted above, while the Y chromosome and mtDNA sequence each occupy a single strand, most of the human genome consists of two strands, which break and recombine. Modelling this process can be difficult, but parallel computing and more powerful processors have made the testing of very complex demographic scenarios tractable. While the Y and mtDNA were a window upon a single line of an individual's ancestors, the whole-genome analyses capture the complex network dynamics of one's whole pedigree.[7]

Whole-genome analyses confirm the broad sketch of Y and mtDNA findings. Africans are the most genetically diverse population, and all non-Africans seem to descend

---

[7]J. Z. Li, D. M. Absher, H. Tang, A. M. Southwick, A. M. Casto, S. Ramachandran & R. M. Myers, 'Worldwide human relationships inferred from genome-wide patterns of variation', *Science, 319* (5866), 2008, pp. 1100–04.

from a branch of ancient Africans. People in Europe tend to be more closely related to others in Europe, people in India tend to be related to people in India, and the Japanese tend to be related to each other.

But all models of the past that utilize the genes of people in the present rely on assumptions. Relatedness is clear in any analysis, but how individuals and populations came to be related in the way they are remains less transparent. Using maternal mtDNA researchers found that South Asians tend to be more related to the people to their east than those to their west.[8] That means that the foremothers of Indians were more closely related to the foremothers of the Chinese, than they were to the foremothers of the Iranians (or other West Eurasians). In contrast, the paternal Y-chromosomal lineages of Indians were more closely related to peoples to the west.[9] But, there were interesting variations in the patterns, with people in the northwest of India and 'upper castes' exhibiting higher proportions of Y chromosomes with West Eurasian affinities.[10]

---

[8]M. Metspalu, T. Kivisild, E. Metspalu, J. Parik, G. Hudjashov, K. Kaldma & P. Endicott, 'Most of the extant mtDNA boundaries in south and southwest Asia were likely shaped during the initial settlement of Eurasia by anatomically modern humans', *BMC genetics*, 5(1), 2004, p. 26.

[9]P. A. Underhill, N. M. Myres, S. Rootsi, M. Metspalu, L. A. Zhivotovsky, R. J. King & I. Kutuev, 'Haplogroup R1a', *European Journal of Human Genetics*, 18(4), 2010, p. 479.

[10]R. S. Wells, N. Yuldasheva, R. Ruzibakiev, P. A. Underhill, I. Evseeva, J. Blue-Smith & K. Balakrishnan, 'The Eurasian heartland: A continental perspective on Y-chromosome diversity', *Proceedings of the National Academy of Sciences*, 98(18), 2001, pp. 10244–49.

The results from genome-wide analyses presented a more nuanced pattern.[11] While the results from mtDNA and Y can be stark and definitive, as they summarize a single lineage, the genome-wide reconstructions shed light on the average patterns of many ancestral pedigrees. On the whole, South Asians occupied a position between West Eurasians and East Eurasians, the former being the people of the Near East and Europe, and the latter of East and Southeast Asia. But this varied by geography and caste. As a rule of thumb, the further north and west a population in South Asia, the genetically closer it is to populations from the Middle East and Europe. Additionally, traditional upper castes such as the Brahmins are also closer to populations from the Middle East and Europe. Scheduled castes and tribal populations had the least affinity to people from the Middle East and Europe. Though these latter groups were not exactly genetically close to people from East and Southeast Asia, their genetic ancestry indicated a deep relationship to East and Southeast Asians.

The interplay between caste and geography can be subtle. Brahmins from Uttar Pradesh and Jats from Punjab both exhibit closer affinity to West Eurasians than Brahmins from Tamil Nadu. But Chamars from Uttar Pradesh exhibit less affinity to West Eurasians than Brahmins from Tamil Nadu. Groups like Reddys and Nadars in South India are both distinct from Scheduled Castes and Scheduled Tribes,

---

[11]D. Reich, K. Thangaraj, N. Patterson, A. L. Price, & L. Singh, 'Reconstructing Indian population history', *Nature*, *461* (7263), 2009, p. 489.

and local Brahmins. In Bengal, the native Brahmins seem genetically closer to Brahmins from Uttar Pradesh than they are to non-Brahmin Bengalis.

Since 2010, a group of Indian and American researchers has constructed a general model to explain these phenomena.[12] The fact that South Asian groups exhibit varied relationships to West Eurasians is due to the fact that all South Asians derive a part of their ancestry from a group very similar to West Eurasians, the 'Ancestral North Indian' (ANI), plus a group distantly related to East Eurasians, the 'Ancestral South Indian' (ASI). As is evident in the nomenclature, the ancestral fractions of the ANI and ASI vary from north to south. Additionally, the researchers realized that of all the groups in eastern Eurasia, the indigenous people of the Andaman Islands were genetically the closest proxy for the historical ASI. This does not mean that the Andamanese were ASI. Rather, they last shared common ancestors with the ASI about 50,000 years ago.

Because admixture between very different populations leaves distinct genetic signatures which attenuate over time, the researchers could conclude that there were pure ASI populations 4,000 years ago, whereas today none remain. Additionally, around 2,000 years ago gene flow between different modern jati groups seems to have stopped. Individuals within a jati began to exclusively marry only

---

[12]P. Moorjani, K. Thangaraj, N. Patterson, M. Lipson, P. R. Loh, P. Govindaraj, & L. Singh, 'Genetic evidence for recent population mixture in India', *The American Journal of Human Genetics*, 93(3), 2013, pp. 422–38.

others from the same jati. This long-term endogamy means that not only are South Asian populations resident in the same region very genetically distinct from one another, with large variations in their ANI/ASI ratio, but they are often quite genetically homogeneous within a group and exhibit unique disease risks.[13]

A model of a two-way mixture between a population with West Eurasian affinities and one that was closer to groups to the east, has held until recently. There were a few exceptions. Bengalis seem to have had substantial admixture from an East Asian population 1,500 years ago.[14] The Austro-Asiatic people of the Chota Nagpur plateau also seem to have an older admixture from East Asians, mediated in particular through migration of males.[15] Other groups, such as Makranis, showed evidence of African admixture.[16] The Parsis seem descended

---

[13]N. Nakatsuka, P. Moorjani, N. Rai, B. Sarkar, A. Tandon, N. Patterson & A. Kaushik, 'The promise of discovering population-specific disease-associated genes in South Asia', *Nature genetics*, *49*(9), 2017, p. 1403.

[14]E. K. Karlsson, J. B. Harris, S. Tabrizi, A. Rahman, I. Shlyakhter, N. Patterson & A. Sheikh, 'Natural selection in a Bangladeshi population from the cholera-endemic Ganges river delta', *Science translational medicine*, 5(192), 192ra86-192ra86, 2013.

[15]Chaubey, Gyaneshwer, et al. 'Population genetic structure in Indian Austroasiatic speakers: the role of landscape barriers and sex-specific admixture', *Molecular Biology and Evolution* 28.2, 2010, pp. 1013–24.

[16]R. Laso-Jadart, C. Harmant, H. Quach, N. Zidane, C. Tyler-Smith, Q. Mehdi & E. Patin, 'The Genetic Legacy of the Indian Ocean Slave Trade: Recent Admixture and Post-admixture Selection in the Makranis of Pakistan', *The American Journal of Human Genetics*, *101*(6), 2017, pp. 977–84.

from recent migrants from Iran.[17]

The initial work with genome-wide analyses established the position of South Asians in the broader scope of Eurasian genetic variation. But it did not establish fine-grained affinities. For the ASI component this was expected, as no modern group was a very good proxy for this population. It did not exist in pure form for thousands of years, but was a 'ghost population', inferred from the genetic data of present-day South Asians.[18] In contrast, several modern populations did not seem to be very different from the ANI. Early research found strong signals of shared ancestry between South Asian groups of varied provenance and peoples from West Asia and East Central Europe, with many groups across South Asia exhibiting similarities to Caucasian Georgians, and some groups, such as the Tiwari Brahmins, exhibiting affinities to ancient samples from Eastern Europe and Central Asia.[19]

But there have long been clues to such external affinities from the Y-chromosomal lineages. Though most South Asian mtDNA lineages are deeply rooted in the subcontinent, one particular Y-chromosomal lineage, R1a1a, has a widespread

[17]G. Chaubey, Q. Ayub, N. Rai, S. Prakash, V. Mushrif-Tripathy, M. Mezzavilla & M. Karmin, 'Like sugar in milk: Reconstructing the genetic history of the Parsi population', *Genome biology*, 18 (1), 110, 2017.

[18]D. Reich, *Who We Are and How We Got Here: Ancient DNA and the New Science of the Human Past.* London: Oxford University Press, 2018.

[19]I. Lazaridis, D. Nadel, G. Rollefson, D. C. Merrett, N. Rohland, S. Mallick & S. Connell, 'Genomic insights into the origin of farming in the ancient Near East', *Nature*, 536(7617), 2016, p. 419.

Eurasian distribution.[20] In particular, R1a1a is found across Eastern Europe, Central Asia, and South Asia. Present at higher frequencies in northwest South Asia and among upper castes, some researchers have suggested that it is evidence of Bronze Age migration from the Eurasian steppe by Indo–Aryans.[21] But other work showed that while East European and Asian lineages of R1a1a could be assigned to two groups, Z280 and Z93, respectively, they could not establish definitively whether Z280 or Z93 were from Europe or South Asia.[22] Both branches are quite homogeneous, rather than having one branch being more notably diverse than the other, and so more likely to be near the point of origin. Y-chromosomal phylogenies are difficult in part because the Y chromosome is a small region of the genome lacking much variation. Those regions of the Y chromosome with a great deal of variation, termed microsatellites, were optimal for diagnostic matches of close relatives, but less useful for evolutionary inference, due to the rapidity with which they changed. But more recently, whole-genome sequencing, where every position along the genome is interrogated has yielded novel results.[23] R1a1a, like several

---

[20]P. A. Underhill, N. M. Myres, S. Rootsi, M. Metspalu, L. A. Zhivotovsky, R. J. King & I. Kutuev, 'Separating the Post-glacial coancestry of European and Asian Y chromosomes within haplogroup R1a', *European Journal of Human Genetics*, *18*(4), 2010, p. 479.

[21]Wells, R. S., op cit., p. 3

[22]Underhill, P. A., op cit., p. 5

[23]Jobling, M. A., & Tyler-Smith, C. (2017). Human Y-chromosome variation in the genome-sequencing era. *Nature Reviews Genetics*, *18*(8), 485.

other Y chromosomal lineages, seems to have expanded from a small ancestral group on the order of 4,000 years ago.[24] This is in contrast to South Asian mtDNA lineages, which are more diverse and clearly deeply rooted in the subcontinent. Some researchers previously skeptical of migration from external sources now posit that a significant influx of mobile male pastoralists brought R1a1a-Z93 to the Indian subcontinent 4,000 years ago.[25] In other words, R1a1a-Z93 in South Asia could be a marker for lineages of Indo–Aryan males who arrived as a 'band of brothers.'

But inference from modern DNA can take us only so far. Since 2010[26] the study of patterns from ancient DNA has revolutionized our understanding of questions as diverse as the peopling of Europe[27] and our relationship to Neanderthals.[28]

---

[24]M. Karmin, L. Saag, M. Vicente, M. A. W. Sayres, M. Järve, U. G. Talas & L. Pagani, 'A recent bottleneck of Y chromosome diversity coincides with a global change in culture', *Genome research*, 2015; G. D. Poznik, Y. Xue, F. L. Mendez, T. F. Willems, A. Massaia, M. A. W. Sayres & Y. Chen, 'Punctuated bursts in human male demography inferred from 1,244 worldwide Y-chromosome sequences', *Nature Genetics*, *48*(6), 2016, p. 593.
[25]M. Silva, M. Oliveira, D. Vieira, A. Brandão, T. Rito, J. B. Pereira & M. Pala, 'A genetic chronology for the Indian Subcontinent points to heavily sex-biased dispersals', *BMC Evolutionary Biology*, *17*(1), 2017, p. 88.
[26]M. Rasmussen, Y. Li, S. Lindgreen, J. S. Pedersen, A. Albrechtsen, I. Moltke & M. Bertalan, 'Ancient human genome sequence of an extinct Palaeo-Eskimo', *Nature*, *463*(7282), 2010, p. 757.
[27]I. Lazaridis, N. Patterson, A. Mittnik, G. Renaud, S. Mallick, K. Kirsanow & B. Berger, 'Ancient human genomes suggest three ancestral populations for present-day Europeans', *Nature*, *513*(7518), 2014, p. 409.
[28]R. E. Green, J. Krause, A. W. Briggs, T. Maricic, U. Stenzel, M. Kircher & N. F. Hansen, 'A draft sequence of the Neandertal genome', *Science*, *328*(5979), 2010, pp. 710–22.

One of the major insights from the study of ancient DNA is that genetic relationships inferred from modern variation are hobbled by limitations because many modern populations represent mixtures between ancestral groups which no longer exist. Europeans, for example, seem to be a fusion of multiple very distinct groups which flourished at the end of the last Ice Age, 11,650 years ago. Only a minority of the ancestry of modern Europeans derives from Pleistocene hunter-gatherers. While in Southern Europe ancestry from Near Eastern farmers[29] is more prominent, in Northern Europe the heritage of Eurasian pastoralists who arrived during the Bronze Age predominates.[30]

Today the ancient DNA evidence from South Asia still remains thin in comparison to that for Western Eurasia. One of the major reasons is no doubt climate (DNA preserves poorly in warmer temperatures). But some findings have already shed light on questions relevant to Indian population-genetic history. Y-chromosomal lineages bearing R1a1a-Z93 were found from graves of the Sbruna culture, which flourished from the Dnieper to the southern reaches of the

---

[29]C. Valdiosera, T. Günther, J. C. Vera-Rodríguez, I. Ureña, E. Iriarte, R. Rodríguez-Varela & L. Rodríguez, 'Four millennia of Iberian biomolecular prehistory illustrate the impact of prehistoric migrations at the far end of Eurasia', *Proceedings of the National Academy of Sciences*, 201717762, 2018. [30]W. Haak, I. Lazaridis, N. Patterson, N. Rohland, S. Mallick, B. Llamas & Q. Fu, 'Massive migration from the steppe was a source for Indo–European languages in Europe', *Nature*, 522(7555), p. 207; M. E. Allentoft, M. Sikora, K. G. Sjögren, S. Rasmussen, M. Rasmussen, J. Stenderup & A. S. Malaspinas, 'Population genomics of bronze age Eurasia', *Nature*, 522(7555), 2015, pp. 167.

Volga Mountains 3,800 to 3,200 years before the present.[31]
These individuals showed no genome-wide evidence of any
distinctively South Asian heritage. That is, ASI ancestry.
This evidence convinced many that R1a1a-Z93 is certainly
intrusive to South Asia, and hailing from the Eurasian steppe.

More recently, two research groups have reported results
on ancient populations liminal to South Asia.[32] Though few
ancient genetic samples from South Asia proper exist, there
are many more from West Asia, Central Asia, and the broad
swath from the Baikal region of Siberia to Eastern Europe.
Additionally, there are ancient samples from the Swat Valley
in Pakistan as well as the Rakhigarhi sample in modern
Indian Punjab, with the latter dating to the mature Harappan
period 4,250 years ago, and the former from the Iron Age.
By comparing a wide range of modern and ancient samples,
some general conclusions are attainable even with the paucity
of ancient South Asian samples.

First, the indigenous component among South Asians,
previously termed ASI, may itself be more complex than
previously thought. As evidenced by deep lineages of mtDNA

[31]I. Mathieson, I. Lazaridis, N. Rohland, S. Mallick, N. Patterson,
S. A. Roodenberg & K. Sirak, 'Eight thousand years of natural selection
in Europe', *BioRxiv*, 016477, 2015.
[32]V. M. Narasimhan, N. J. Patterson, P. Moorjani, I. Lazaridis, L. Mark,
S. Mallick & I. Olalde, 'The Genomic Formation of South and Central
Asia. *bioRxiv*, 292581, 2018; P. de Barros Damgaard, R. Martiniano, J.
Kamm, J. V. Moreno-Mayar, G. Kroonen, M. Peyrot & V. Zaibert, 'The
first horse herders and the impact of early Bronze Age steppe expansions
into Asia', *Science*, eaar7711, 2018.

haplogroup M, South Asians clearly have an ancestral component deeply diverged and distinct from those of peoples of the Near East and Europe, which tend to be of macrohaplogroup N. And yet this ancestry is also very distinct from that of most modern East and Southeast Asians. The closest genetic proxies for ASI are the Negrito peoples of western Southeast Asia and the Andaman Islands. But these groups are still not particularly close genetically to the indigenous peoples of Pleistocene South Asia. Though researchers have only yet seen through the glass darkly in regards to the nature of the ASI.

A deeper analysis of the affinities of ASI has revealed that in fact this construct harbors within it about 25 per cent West Eurasian ancestry.[33] The West Eurasian ancestry itself seems directly tied to West Asian farmers from the environs of modern Iran. The ASI were a compound of these farmers along with indigenous South Asians, 'Ancient Ancestral South Indians', or AASI. They, along with many South Asian peoples, especially those from South India, seem to lack the steppe component of ancestry associated with R1a1a-Z93.

This steppe ancestry has deep affinities with late Neolithic and early Bronze Age populations which were dominant along the western portion of the Eurasian forest-steppe zone. A broad zone of related peoples was defined by the Andronovo and Sintashta cultures on its eastern fringe, who expanded from the west 4,000 years ago into Central Asia. Ancient DNA confirms that these groups were the ones bearing

---

[33] V. M. Narasimhan, op cit., p. 7.

Y-chromosomal haplogroup R1a1a-Z93, and this ancestry is today widespread in the zone from Iran into northern South Asia. But, within India proper it is particularly apparent among Brahmin groups. The results from the Swat Valley, as well as the Harappan-era Rakhigarhi sample, seem to argue that the steppe ancestry within South Asia likely dates to after 2000 BCE.

In contrast, the West Eurasian ancestry associated with Iranian agriculturalists is found across all caste groups and the whole subcontinent. It is also present in Harappan-era individuals as is suggested by the recent results from Rakhigarhi. Just as the ASI were more complex than previously thought, ANI itself also contains multitudes. The genetic profile of the Indus Valley Civilization (IVC) is that of an ancient admixture between incoming agriculturalists from Iran and AASI. These people contributed to 70 per cent of the ancestry of the ANI, the balance of which was bolstered by the arrival of pastoralists from the steppe after 2000 BCE.[34] Though even within this society there seems to have been variation in ancestry, as the Rakhigarhi individual seems more skewed toward ASI ancestry, like South Indian scheduled tribes, while the peripheral samples had more Iranian farmer ancestry.

Ancient DNA from Afghanistan, Tajikistan, and South Asia all seem to indicate that the genetic intrusion of Central Asian pastoralists dates to the period after 2000 BCE. Culturally this corresponds to the arrival of chariots in the

---

[34]V. M. Narasimhan, op cit., p. 7

Near East,[35] as well as the attestation around 1750 BCE of an Indo–Aryan group in the Upper Euphrates basin as part of the ruling class of the Mitanni state.[36]

Because the period before 500 BCE is preliterate in most of the world there is only so much we can say in regards to ethnolinguistic identities. Even groups known to history such as the Kassite rulers of Babylonia have shadowy affinities, in part due to the dominance of written languages such as Akkadian, which had the effect of masking oral diversity and identity. Geneticists cannot assert definitively that particular peoples spoke particular languages. Genetic inference and ancient DNA can only establish affinities, and propose models of demographic change.

What geneticists can say is that the expansion of R1a1a-Z93, which is common among Central Asians and upper castes in South Asia, seems to have occurred after about 2000 BCE. That it spread with steppe pastoralists from the Volga region as they pushed south and east seems the most likely hypothesis. Additionally, ancestral components which are associated with these steppe people arrived around the same period from Afghanistan into Pakistan and India. And interestingly, the variant of lactase persistence, the ability to digest milk sugar as an adult, found in modern northwest

---

[35]D. F. Easton, 'Indo–European Takeovers-Drews Robert: The Coming of the Greeks: Indo–European Conquests in the Aegean and the Near East. pp. xviii, 257; 8 figs', Cambridge: Cambridge University Press, 1988. *The Classical Review*, *41*(1), pp. 132–33.

[36]P. E. Dumont, 'Indo–Aryan names from Mitanni, Nuzi, and Syrian documents', *Journal of the American Oriental Society*, 1947, pp. 251–53.

India is the same as that found in Northern Europe.[37]

We know from archaeology that in the centuries after 2000 BCE the Harappan society went into sharp decline, as Indian civilization became less urban and simpler. The results from the Swat Valley in Pakistan date to a later period: after 900 BCE down to the historical period. And they show an interesting dynamic. The earliest samples have a minority of steppe ancestry, on the order of 20 per cent. The balance is similar to the ancestry of the IVC-related samples, a mix of Iranian agriculturalist and AASI. As time progresses the fraction of both steppe and AASI ancestry increases in the Swat Valley.

The genetic evidence for endogamy in South Asia today is striking, with highly structured regional populations. As noted earlier this seems to have crystallized on the order of 2,000 years before the present. But the genetic evidence also points to a massive episode of mixing after the decline of the IVC and the historical period. The steppe ancestry is intrusive across South Asia to the period after 2000 BCE, but groups which are highly enriched for this ancestry in comparison to Iranian agriculturalist heritage, such as North Indian Brahmins, also have a greater fraction of AASI ancestry than populations to the west.[38]

At the current moment the genetic data from

---

[37]I. Gallego Romero, C. Basu Mallick, A. Liebert, F. Crivellaro, G. Chaubey, Y. Itan & D. Reich, 'Herders of Indian and European cattle share their predominant allele for lactase persistence', *Molecular biology and evolution*, *29*(1), 2011, pp. 249–60.
[38]V. M. Narasimhan, op cit., p. 7.

contemporary populations in South Asia is copious. Researchers can make strong and definitive assertions about particular jati groups, and regional population clusters.[39] But drawing inferences about past historical events from contemporary patterns of variation is often more difficult, and only the most general claims can rely on contemporary data alone.

The differences between steppe populations, and Neolithic-period agriculturalists from Iran, or the complex demographic origins of the ASI, will come into sharp and indisputable focus with ancient DNA, which brings ghost populations back to life. This is the pattern which holds for Europe and the Near East, as dozens, and even hundreds, of ancient individuals allow researchers to create detailed models of migration across thousands of years. Fine-grained insight cannot be built upon only a few samples.

The genetic patterns around the fringes of South Asia are now well understood. The recent arrival of steppe pastoralists from the steppe bearing R1a1a-Z93 into the highland zone to the north and west of the Indian subcontinent in the period after 2000 BC now seems assured. The few samples we do have from the mature-phase IVC indicate that this ancestry was absent in South Asia during this period. We also see today that steppe ancestry is present at much higher fractions among upper castes, and in groups in the north of India and in Pakistan.

All this evidence strongly points to the arrival of a

---

[39]N. Nakatsuka, op cit., p. 3.

group of pastoralist Indo–European speakers to South Asia in the period after 2000 BCE. We know these pastoralists were Indo–European speakers, because literate civilization persisted continuously in the Near East, and Indo–Aryans are attested in the historical record from Mesopotamia in the first half of the second millennium BCE.[40]

Until more ancient DNA results are reported from India the temporal and spatial details of how these pastoralists spread across South Asia in the centuries after their arrival will be highly conjectural. Many groups in south and east India show little impact from the steppe pastoralists. And yet these populations also exhibit fascinating variation which hints at unexpected histories. The India that the people from the steppe expanded into was not a homogeneous formless whole, but already textured by its own complexities. The Indo–Aryans were only the latest of the prehistoric migrations to leave their mark upon the mosaic of South Asian genetic ancestry. Solving the mystery of their origins and arrival is only the opening chapter, not the conclusion.

---

[40]P. E. Dumont, op cit., p. 9.

AFTERWORD

ROMILA THAPAR

We have seen from the previous chapters that there is a diversity of evidence for this phase of early history and the possibility therefore of more than a single interpretation and the opportunity to ask many questions. It is problematic to attempt a single uniformly applicable answer that integrates and encompasses all the evidence. Nor is a single answer likely since the geographical area is vast and the time bracket huge. There was much historical change during what is called the Vedic period of Indian history. It might, therefore, be worth considering fresh ways of looking at the evidence that would enhance our understanding of this segment of the past. What is clear from the evidence is the necessity to demarcate that which circulates as popular ideas about 'the Aryans', readily publicized through both the media and various public organizations and people, not to mention some of the content of textbooks, on the one hand, and on the other, from the research that is being done through a range of scholarly and scientific work. In 1969, when I first wrote on the subject as an historian, I referred to the 'Aryan Question' as a red herring. It remains that on many public fora but less so in scholarly circles.

The multiplicity of popular views, many unaware of

historical evidence, reflects the kind of confusion that a rationally ordered history has to confront. The confusion, as is widely known, has less to do with the evidence from the past, and more with the fact that what is claimed as history is an essential requirement in legitimizing a political ideology, even if the supposedly historical narrative is unacceptable to most historians. It is also grist to the imagination of those who write fiction and as fiction is best left to them. But this is not what historical reconstruction is built on. One does get exhausted with having to constantly reiterate the fact that the writing of history has to follow what is now a recognized methodology of historical research. This is based on using evidence that is known to be reliable, on causality that observes logical connections, and on rational argument.

There is therefore now a tendency towards a bifurcation of views on the Vedic period. The theory of indigenous origin and a singular evolution is heavily propagated by various agencies that claim to be religio-cultural organizations, and by the present Indian government, and by those who are currently preparing textbooks for the central and state financed schools and others under the aegis of the government. There are also a few archaeologists and historians who endorse the theory but their arguments are slight and repetitive, and in the absence of analysis, don't move much beyond some nineteenth century interpretations.

The other view contradicts the above. It is held by a substantial body of professional archaeologists and historians of South Asia, both Indian and non-Indian, who find the above views unacceptable, and have found both the attempts to suggest the evidence for them and the logic of the arguments in support of them, unconvincing. They do not endorse the notion that there existed a single dominant Aryan culture from the pre-Harappan times to the turn of the first millennium CE, nor that this culture was untouched by anyone from outside the subcontinent.

The work of archaeologists and historians has been going on apace which is why the existing evidence is so important. This will enable us to ask more relevant questions using the data for this period of history, and move away from what have been some rather dead-end questions. Provided, of course, that we are not prevented from doing so.

The context to these questions is that what we call the Vedic period was a phase of early Indian history that registered historical change, bookended as it were, by the decline of one civilization in the Indus plain and the rise of another in the Ganga plain. It was therefore a period of many changes and both these and their nuances need to be ferreted out and analysed. Nor is it a period when the world outside the subcontinent was barred entry. On the contrary many winds blew through the Indian landscape and many people entered and settled.

The answer to the question of origins lies in first defining what categories constitute that which we call 'the Aryan'. We need to ask whether the Vedic culture in itself was a uniform entity or whether there were differentiations, each with its own creativity, that need to be examined, turn by turn. Fortunately, the serious side to the study, stemming from research and scholarship has grown, and as the previous chapters show, there is also now the presence of other disciplines that are providing what may be new sources of information. These inevitably raise further questions, ranging from population migrations to patterns of living.

The public debate may well continue and believe what it wishes to believe, but the research on the subject is seeking to answer more appropriate and pertinent questions. We are familiar with the work on Vedic texts by excellent Sanskrit scholars some of whose writing has played a dynamic role in taking forward these studies. That continues, but now there is also the juxtaposition of the results of other related studies, and also the contribution from some unexpected disciplines that are providing a different kind of evidence, some of which has been discussed in this book. We also have to keep time and space in mind. This history relates to a period that extends to over a millennium—from 1500 to 500 BCE—and geographically covers the northern half of the subcontinent from the Himalayas to the northern Deccan. Given the natural diversity of this space as well as of its populations there can be no simple uniform answers.

The questions that are presently engaging the attention of scholars are many but some seem more significant. I would like to mention a couple since they emerge from the kind of evidence that was discussed in the previous chapters. One of course is, that with the recognition of the close proximity of non-Aryan and Aryan, the processes by which elements of the one entered the other and the forms that this took, have to be investigated. The presence of the former is evident from the various sources. There are references to interactions of diverse kinds between the two that we have to recognize. This would require more flexibility in our vision of this period than we have assumed so far. The non-Aryan may seem invisible but a careful re-examination of the texts points to visibility. This question is difficult to answer since such links are not immediately apparent, and one may have to delve beyond the obvious in any search for these.

The focus has so far been on attempting to define the Aryanism of the Vedic texts as fundamental to the understanding of early India, and to the forms it took in later periods. However, it would be as well to recognize that whoever claimed to be Aryan in whatever form, had to contend with or accommodate whatever was non-Aryan in their midst. This process did not consist of just the dominance of the one, but also included its interface with the other. It is significant that the questioning of Vedic Brahmanism surfaces by the mid-first millennium BCE, in the many new dharmas associated with the Shramanic and similar sects.

The second question requires recognizing that the cultures which evolve are not just Vedic but reflect the cultures within the subcontinent, and those that were outside of what we regard as boundaries of the subcontinent. Some straddled these boundaries. The cultures depicted in Old Iranian and Indo–Aryan texts—the *Avesta* and the *Rig Veda*—were not alien to each other and have to be seen as closely interconnected. Where Old Iranian mentions Airiia, Indo–Aryan mentions Arya. This makes what is today defined as indigenous or foreign for that period, ineffective.

Cultures of any consequence do not evolve in isolation.

They constantly react to what surrounds them and are aware of what they have to control if they are to retain their power, or what they lose when bereft of power. The cultures of this space and time were not confined to the nineteenth century borders based on cartography and modern politics, within which we have tried to hold them. Cultures in frontier regions were in any case always in continuous contact with those further away. We have to recognize this communication as part of our history as well. The use of Indo–Aryan or its cognates was not restricted to India. Parallels from Indo-Iranian, the Mitanni Indo–Aryan in Anatolia, or among the Kassites in Babylonia, do not allow us to confine our sights to the subcontinent. How Indo–Aryan made a sudden and brief appearance in the latter two areas and then faded out entirely has yet to be explained. But what it does point to is that the history of Indo–Aryan in India was part of the larger history of western Eurasia.

The hymns of the *Rig Veda* were eventually recorded in written form, many centuries after they were composed, having been preserved through being meticulously memorized in remarkable ways. The recensions date to the early first millennium BCE, and the one that has current usage is by Shakalya. The hymns date to different periods, and beyond a broad identification of some that are early and some that are late, a more precise date is awaited.

In the geographical spread of Indo–Aryan, initially across the northern half of the subcontinent, the degree of dissemination in each area would have been different. The existing populations in these areas were not identical. The geographical spread as given in the Vedic corpus begins with an initial area that coincides with a part of the Harappan geography, but effectively the larger geographies of each cover different regions. The geography of the later Vedas extends eastwards from the Punjab and the Doab into less familiar areas. The Harappan geography looks south to Gujarat and the Gulf and then westwards to Mesopotamia, driven not by migrations but by trade—copper and lapis lazuli probably being the more lucrative cargo. This geographical orientation is important if we are to locate the gaze of the Harappans and their systems of knowledge. The decline of this contact would have coincided with the decline of the Harappan cities. The urbanization of the Ganga plain does not repeat the pattern of Harappan urbanization. Harappan continuities are difficult to trace in the material culture. If they are to be sought they will have to be searched for in other ways. Some oral traditions and place names may have continuity even if of a limited kind. This will be the subject of research when the Harappan language is known and the pictograms on the seals understood.

A basic question is that of the meaning of the word Arya and Aryan, both used as a label and as a qualifier. Does the label refer to a language, or to a descent group, or to a cultural form linked to specific mores and religious connotations, or is it used simply as a qualifier indicating those that are respected? Are these differentiated meanings used in different historical periods or simultaneously? Did the meaning change on being applied to diverse people at different points of time? The term is not restricted to India.

The Achaemenid king, Darius, in an inscription refers to himself as Arya and refers to the inscription as being written in Aryan. We know that a large variety of people of different origins were, in later history, called Arya-putra because of their status. For the same reason the high status Rakshasas and Vanaras address each other as Arya. Ravana refers to himself and his ministers as Aryas. The term Anarya is applied to various clan members when they behave in what are thought to be unethical ways. According to one Purana, followers of the Shramana religions are said to be Anaryas and Daityas, and therefore fit to be done away with by Shiva.[1]

In the Buddhist texts, that which is of worth is given the epithet of Ariya (Pali for Arya) such as the four Ariya Sacca (Four Noble Truths). Reference is made to the Yavanas and the Kambojas located in the north-west who are said to have just two varnas, the Arya and the Dasa, but there is flexibility between them and each can become the other (*Majjhima Nikaya* II. 149). It is interesting that the same two terms are used as in the *Rig Veda*, but obviously the meaning has changed. The Anaryas in these texts are those who contradict the Buddhist teaching. This is an inversion of what the *Dharmashastras* say.

Jaina texts also comment on this qualifier. The Ariya confronts the Anariya who is also called Milakkhu, a version of Mleccha. The Ariya is known by nine characteristics that

---

[1] J. Bronkhorst and M. M. Deshpande (eds.), *Aryan and non-Aryan in South Asia: Evidence, Interpretation and Ideology,* Cambridge, Massachusetts: Harvard University Press, 1999.

include birth, region, occupation, language, and behaviour.[2] The Jaina religion is the Ariya Dhamma, and others are Anariya. The languages in which it is taught include those excluded by Brahmana teachers. Castes low in the *Dharmashastras* and some referred to as Anarya, are here said to be Arya. The Aryavarta or the land of the Aryas shifts marginally in geographical coverage from the Brahmanical, to the Buddhist, to the Jaina texts.

One of the questions that we have to address is how did the Indo–Aryan based languages—Sanskrit, Pali, and various Prakrits—become the pre-eminent languages in the northern subcontinent. Interestingly, by about the mid-first millennium BCE there develops a differentiation among them. Vedic Sanskrit is not identical with the Sanskrit that is used for other texts, a distinction recorded by Panini. The Buddhist texts of the first millennium are written in Pali, and the Jaina texts in Prakrit. Prakrit seems to have been almost a lingua franca during that millennium since a range of inscriptions are composed in Prakrit. The version of Prakrit in each inscription reflects a recognized regional variation—for example in one version of Ashoka's Prakrit edict the 'r' sound is replaced by the 'l' sound, and 'raja' becomes 'laja'. Some of these later variations were earlier referred to in Vedic texts as characteristic of the Mleccha, their language being faulty, but later they are normal.

As we have seen earlier, the *Rig Veda* differentiates between the Arya varna and the Dasa varna as two distinct

---

[2]Ibid.

groups, and in further descriptions emphasizes the difference in language, religion and culture. Language was a strong marker. The Dasa was seen as what we today would call 'the Other'. The Dasas are not Aryas and how the two relate to each other, varies. Confrontation between the two is referred to in an earlier hymn of the *Rig Veda* (2.12) in which Indra is said to have vanquished the Dasas and smashed the Dasyus, but a hymn in one of its late books is more reconciliatory with mention of the two varnas. (1.179.6.). This could be a coincidence.

But curiously, as it has been pointed out, reference is also made to the Dasi-putra Brahmanas. Who were these? Did Dasi refer to a woman of the society of the Other, or to the woman who worked in the home of the householder and was considered of low status and was expected to provide a variety of services. One is reminded of the story of Satyakama Jabala the young student who comes to study with the teacher Gautama. When asked for his gotra on the assumption that he was a Brahmana, he replies that he does not know who his father was because his mother worked as a maid in a household where many men came and went. Gautama's comment is that he must be a Brahmana because he told the truth. (*Chhandogya Upanisad* 4.4.1–5).

Another text of the Vedic corpus refers to a son of a Dasi, Kavasha Ailusha. The Brahmanas at first regarded him with contempt because of his birth and sent him away. But when he prayed to the river Sarasvati and the river came to him, they not only accepted him but declared him to be the best among them (*Aitareya Brahmana* VIII.1.; *Kaushitaki*

Brahmana 12.1. 3). Some were mentioned as respected rishis in the *Rig Veda*. Occasionally the mother's name is also given, as in the name of Kakshivant Aushija, the son of Dirghatamas Mamateya whose mother was a Dasi, Ushij (*Brihad-devata* 4.11 ff.). Yet they were not called Aryas, nor were they called Mleccha, although they obviously knew the Aryan language well. Curiously some of the hymns of the late Book Ten of the *Rig Veda* are attributed to a well-known Kavasha who may well have been Kavasha Ailusha. The hymns indicate that the author was close to the families of the chiefs of clans. Since these hymns are in the late book of the *Rig Veda* there would have been time enough for some Dasi-putras to have become proficient in the Vedic compositions and thus qualify to be called Brahmanas. In this process some of their rituals did enter the mainstream.

Linguistics tells us that there are elements of Dravidian, and even some Munda, in the language of the Vedas. The list of such words is of considerable interest in terms of reconstructing cultures. A large number of the loanwords in the *Rig Veda* relate to agriculture, which makes good sense.[3] For pastoralists agriculture is not primary but it would have been for the earlier urban centres in need of agricultural support. Would this suggest a process of acculturation between non-Aryan and Aryan speakers? The latter, as migrants—from the steppes or from Punjab going east—came into contact with non-Aryan speakers in various ways: through a relationship of pastoral-agrarian symbiosis;

---

[3]F. B. J. Kuiper, *Aryans in the Rigveda*, Amsterdam: Editions Rodopi, 1991.

or settling in the same area and gradually working together in diverse occupations; or jointly facing the vagaries of ecological change in the area; or intermarrying; or inducting local specialists into the society that claimed authority. That forms of Indo–Aryan became dominant could suggest that their speakers were of a large enough number, or else had access to cultural items that gave them the possibility of attaining a powerful position.

Did the languages spoken by the Dasas become the substratum languages subordinated to the language of the dominant group, or was there perhaps some degree of bilingualism? If this can be investigated, then there would also be the possibility of examining possible traces of Harappan continuities from earlier cultures in north-western India. The most likely continuities would be in the occasional place names, rendered directly or translated from the original word;[4] or as has been suggested in an element of ritual,[5] or in some of the technologies.[6] The latter is suggested for instance, in what is thought to be the more extensive use of iron than of copper, or in the introduction of the horse and chariot to replace the ox cart. Historians have drawn attention to the function of these latter items. This interface may be

---

[4]R. Thapar, 'A Possible Identification of Meluhha', Dilmun and Makan, *Origin Myths and the Early Indian Historical Tradition*, 1978, reprinted in R. Thapar, *Cultural Pasts*, New Delhi: Oxford University Press, 2000, pp. 272–309, 754–81.

[5]I. Mahadevan, 'The Unicorn and the Sacred Filter Standard', *International Journal of Dravidian Linguistics*, 46, 1, 2017, pp. 35–69.

[6]R. S. Sharma, *Advent of the Aryans in India*, Delhi: Manohar, 2001.

speculative at this moment, but if explored with appropriate questions may provide useful pointers. What would the context be if the evidence for non-Aryan societies as given in the Vedic texts were to be collected and correlated with the other sources? In other words, could we try and see the historical context from a different perspective.

Had archaeology provided evidence of a dominant culture with a genesis in north-western India but spreading across northern India in the late second millennium BCE that might have given us a clue. The Harappan culture is geographically demarcated and does not extend beyond the western edges of the Ganga plain. Its contacts are also to the south-west and these do not figure in the *Rig Veda*. If excavations were being carried out in the regions to the west of the borderlands, new evidence may be found, as for instance from what was Elam (south-west Iran), as has been suggested. But such investigations are on hold for the present.

Given that an active urban civilization controlled the entire Indus plain together with its tributaries and a few areas further afield on its edges, would it have disappeared completely with the decline of its cities, even if the reasons for its decline may have been radical ecological changes, and, or a decline in trade with the west? Would there not have been some traces of continuities either in cultures that were its contemporaries or in cultures with which there was a slight overlap? This again can be dismissed as speculation but it could be speculation of a kind that might be conducive to asking more searching questions.

The archaeological picture of the second

millennium BCE is that of diverse scattered cultures spread across the subcontinent. None of them so far has shown signs of being closely connected with the earlier Harappan. Nevertheless some possibilities could be investigated. One would be the few sites, but unfortunately too few, where there is evidence of an overlap between the Late Harappan and the Painted Grey Ware cultures in the north. Can the nature of this overlap be examined in further detail? The second is the contemporaneity of the Late Harappan and the Black and Red Ware sites in parts of Gujarat however short it might have been. The sites are culturally distinct but was there the possibility of some communication? It would involve not just recording material objects but asking more searching questions about the sites. In both cases it would be the tailing off of urban cultures being perhaps in some limited dialogue with small settlements.

The geographical area covered by the Vedic corpus begins with the north-west and the Punjab and moves to the Ganga plain down to the Vindhyas—the area that later in the *Dharmashastra* of Manu is defined as Aryavarta. Mapping place-names and their chronology may provide clues to migrations within the subcontinent, to be compared with those mentioned in the texts, such as that of Videgha Mathava travelling east from the Doab (*Shatapatha Brahmana* 1.4.1.10 ff). Population movements into areas previously settled would bring about some changes in the main language used. These would be the outcome of interaction with speakers of other languages, different from changes that result from the normal evolution of a language. That there were changes in the main language is evident from the need for etymologies and grammars, pre-eminent amongst which were the *Nirukta* of Yaska and the *Ashtadhyayi* of Panini.

What archaeology indicates is that North India was an area of diverse cultures and ecological zones. Some were conducive to breeding cattle and horses and cultivating wheat and barley, whereas others were given to buffalo-herding and rice cultivation. Migrating from one to the other would in itself have required much readjustment. Some populations would have spoken variant languages others would have adapted Indo–Aryan to their own needs. There would be different kinship systems that would have to be sorted out to find a median if thought necessary. This may have led to some divergence in the texts.

There is little data available even of an impressionistic kind on the approximate numbers involved. How large or small were the groups of migrants moving from one area to another or the size of settlements of existing populations that they met with? The archaeological picture suggests small settlements for the second millennium BCE, the evolution of towns in the Ganga plain being later. The migration into north-western India would not have been the sudden entry of hordes sweeping across the country. Migration in most cases, and certainly in this case, appears to be of smaller numbers and over a longer period of time, given the evidence pointing to interaction. Possibly a few clans would have migrated from time to time.[7] The most frequent social unit mentioned in

---

[7]S. Ratnagar, 'Does Archaeology Hold the Answer' in Bronkhorst, J and

the *Rig Veda* is that of clans, sometimes with their location. A comparison of data from the *Rig Veda* with later texts has provided information of migrations in northern India. Much time is required and a period of coexistence for a language to change even marginally and cultures to interact. Migrations need not have followed a single route and there are many possible routes into northern India from beyond the borders.

Among rituals, those linked to the disposal of the dead are another source of information. The Harappan system was that of burial in graves located in cemeteries in the vicinity of cities. This gave way to cremation among elite cultures in post-Vedic times. The Vedic texts sometimes describe burial as an Asura practice. As such it was not approved of, although they do provide details about the graves.[8] This may suggest that this practice might have continued in a limited way until a little later. Graves fade out in the north but remain a central feature in the Megalithic cultures of the peninsula. The nature of these Megalithic cultures, such as those of the Kaveri valley, and some in the Vindhyan region, being so different raise other questions.

Attempts have been made to find the origins of the icons of later Hinduism—such as its deities—in some of the objects that have surfaced at Harappan sites. This seems procedurally problematic. Some of the earliest objects where

---

M. M. Deshpande (eds.), *Aryan and non-Aryan in South Asia: Evidence, Interpretation and Ideology,* Cambridge, Massachusetts: Harvard University Press, 1999.

[8]R. Thapar, 'The Archaeological Background to the Agnicayana Ritual', in F. Staal et al. (eds.), *Agni,* Berkeley: University of California Press, 1983.

they survived, may have remained part of the substratum religion, the objects of worship and practices of the non-elite, referred to as the Shudras in the varna system, and ignored in the texts. Other objects and ideas could have originated in the earlier culture and been inducted into Puranic Hinduism with new attributes and functions. Linear continuities may not be obvious, whereas tracing the reformulations of icons and ideas if possible would be more worthwhile.

In the earlier studies of the Vedic corpus there was much interest in comparative studies of Vedic mythology with other Indo–European mythologies. The search was both for parallels and for the subsequent evolution or deviations in narratives. R. N. Dandekar worked out a methodology that was seminal, and particularly so from a historical perspective.[9] He argued that mythology is neither static nor finite but responds to its context. Myths are better studied in the context of time and space, as also their changes. The personalities and attributes of deities mutated and the relationships among them were governed by culture-historical compulsions. It is often said that the activities of deities could present the ideal form envisaged by the existing society, or else could contradict it. In theory, this choice was that of the deities, but in effect it was the vision of the society concerned. Dandekar drew attention to the concept of dual divinities in the *Rig Veda*. The earliest of these was Mitra–Varuna, cosmic deities that went back to the settlement in the Bactrian region. Could

---

[9]R. N. Dandekar, *Vedic Mythological Tracts*, Delhi: Ajanta Publications, 1979.

this also have to do with their centrality in the Old Iranian sources? When a hero-god was required it was Indra that surfaced. In an interface between cultures, deities and myths would also have been drawn from these diverse sources.

The myths and deities associated with Indo–European cultures were not common to all such cultures, although some were similar. A ritual common to the Indo–Aryan and Old Iranian speakers, but not elsewhere, was that of Soma as it was called by the first group, and Hoama by the second. This further strengthens the closeness between the two groups. The ritual was elaborate, consisting of pressing and consuming the juice of the plant at the site of the sacrifice, accompanied by recitations. The identification of the plant has been subjected to various searches but remains uncertain. Earlier it was thought that it could be an intoxicant, a later suggestion was that it might have been a hallucinogen. Mushrooms and ephedra have been the objects of enquiry. Was the ritual limited to the places where the plant was available? Or did it have a history going back to an earlier time, and perhaps reflective of Shamanism in the region?

Ritual texts have been analysed both to reconstruct the rituals and explain them and also to see them as sources in analysing aspects of society and culture. If the rituals were all performed by those who identified themselves as Aryas, then how does one explain the presence of those Dasas—such as Bribu and Balbutha—who were also patrons of the rituals and acknowledged as such by the Brahmanas? Did they introduce fragments of their own ritual into what was being performed for them? The Dasi-putra Brahmanas, for instance, are likely to have claimed the efficacy of their own rituals and probably included some.

Among the scientific disciplines that are beginning to be called upon in reconstructing the history of this period, one is hydrology, in this case the study of river courses and sources of water. There is a controversy over whether the Sarasvati River referred to in the *Rig Veda* is a reference to the impressive Haraxvaiti—the Iranian name of the river in the Helmand basin—which it could well be with proximity to the Indus system, or whether it was the same as what is now a minor river in Haryana, the Ghaggar that may originally have been part of the large and impressive Hakra system. The interchange of 'h' and 's' in ancient Iranian and Sanskrit names, occurs in other place—names as well, as in Hindu[sh]/Sindhu, and Harayu/Sarayu. It is feasible to suggest that initially the river was Haraxvaiti, and with the migration eastwards, the same name rendered as Sarasvati was applied to the more easterly river. The latter would not have been an impressive river by the mid-second millennium, with a major part having been lost, it is thought, in a tectonic movement. But the memory of the Haraxvaiti may still have coloured the imagination. People tend to repeat names and give old names to new places, rivers, hills, etc., in memory of where they have come from. Was this the reason for repeating the names of rivers?

There is some difference of opinion on whether these rivers were monsoon-fed or snow-fed, the difference being tied to the volume of water. This in turn relates to tracking river courses. The Satlej has a rather problematic history, having changed its course more than once, but others remain relatively stable. Tracking these changes may provide some evidence for explaining shifting settlements.

In the last couple of decades there has been some focus on evidence from an entirely different source and an entirely different discipline: studies in genetics using DNA. Currently the use of this data as a source for history in India is controversial, with some preferring to ignore it, and others arguing that if it proves to be reliable it could introduce some precision in the study of population movements in the subcontinent during past times. Those that reject it sometimes see the DNA idea carrying the baggage of race. The label of R1a comes from DNA. Whether it is called 'Aryan' or not, its presence in the DNA evidence indicates the presence of a Central Asian people in the north Indian population at that time.

There are other problems related to samples taken from ancient burials and such like, as these require a particularly careful prior examination. Samples have to be free of contamination and this can be problematic in warm humid climates. This problem has cropped up at a couple of sites in the northern subcontinent. There also has to be a sufficiently large sample since generalizations made on a single sample could be defective. And preferably the sample should be close to, the period for which it is being examined.

What would perhaps increase the value of this data would be if the DNA patterns once identified were to be mapped separately from other kinds of information and identities. There would then be a clearer picture of population movements and migrations, within a chronological framework. This would mean omitting the superimposition of other identities to begin with, and observing what emerges from the genetic material, evidence from an altogether different discipline. Subsequently the results could be compared with the data from other sources such as archaeology and linguistics. There has been criticism of what has been called the 'tyranny of the texts' by archaeologists from elsewhere, when there has been a rush to fix labels from texts onto archaeological data and then the data is read in accordance with the texts. This could refer to the tendency to label every new excavated culture as 'the Aryans', as was the trend earlier. The evidence from different sources has to be initially viewed separately or studied in a comparative way, until such time as links may be found.

In a more recent study of the DNA material worldwide referred to in the previous chapters, populations in different parts of the world have been examined and the results published for discussion. A section on the Indian subcontinent is also available.[10] Two major groups have been identified and these have been labelled as the Ancestral South Indians (ASI), and the Ancestral North Indians (ANI). The ASI is made up of a population of indigenous hunter-gatherers of India with a mix of farmers from Iran. The ANI, dated to about 4,500 years before the present, has an additional presence of people from the Central Asian steppes. The ANI

---

[10]D. Reich, *Who We Are and How We Got Here*, New York: Oxford University Press, 2018.

carry the genetic marker of R1a also present from an earlier date in neighbouring areas just to the north of Iran and India.

Migrations in past times were frequent but of small groups of people. Bordering areas are particularly open to migrants and more so if there is an exchange nexus involving both sides. There would have been many groups of migrants coming into north-west India. As migrants they presumably came with their own cultural baggage as all migrants do. The population of the north-west was clearly a mixed population of those previously settled there and of migrants. Conceding the fact that the population was mixed and came from three sources—as identified so far—lays the ground for arguing that the emergent culture should be seen as being not uninfluenced by the interface of a variety of belief-systems, languages and patterns of living, emanating from the peoples involved. What resulted was not the creation of a singular monolithic culture characterized by a uniformity such as we have tended to project in the Vedic culture, but clusters of variant cultures, most of which had some interconnections, but were not necessarily identical.

Admittedly the evidence from genetic studies is tantalizing. It would seem to answer some significant questions. It is the application of the evidence from one discipline to help solve problems in another. The kind of data it provides could be useful as a new way of studying particular aspects of certain societies and the people who belonged to them. It could change or confirm, to some extent, our existing formulations about some aspects of the past, depending as always on the reliability of the evidence, and it will add other dimensions to our present studies. At this point we should neither treat it as an old discarded theory in a new garb, nor as an unchallengeable fact. We must do what we do with all knowledge, whether continuing from the past or new, namely, examine it carefully, observe its evolution, and constantly assess its viability—and more so when further along even newer knowledge marks a presence, as is bound to happen—provided it is not suppressed.

These approaches might broaden our vision into accepting the fact that cultures in a region since the beginning of time have interacted with each other. New cultures emerge from these interactions that do not necessarily discard the old but allow them to mutate or fade away if need be. In the nineteenth century when the concept of civilizations was crucial to historical thinking, there was almost an obsession to claim a particular civilization as the oldest and project it as essentially self-created, uniform and singular. Today civilizations are seen as porous and dependent on each other. What the evidence from various sources does point to is that the second millennium BCE in northern India was a period of much interaction both among communities within the subcontinent, with neighbours across the borders, and with groups of migrants filtering in. It was in this interaction that there lay the genesis of impressive cultural articulations of the time.

ACKNOWLEDGEMENTS

The title of this book was first used for an essay by Romila Thapar that was published in *Seminar* magazine.

A version of 'The Search for the Aryans' and 'Multiple Theories about the "Aryan"' by Romila Thapar were first published in *The Aryan: Recasting Constructs* published by Three Essays Collective in 2008.

A version of 'The Complications of Genetics' by Kai Friese was first published in *India Today*.

Jaya Menon would like to thank Supriya Varma for her incisive comments on the essay entitled 'In the Aftermath of the Harappan Period (*c.* 2000–500 BCE)'.

NOTES ON THE CONTRIBUTORS

Romila Thapar is Emeritus Professor of History at the Jawaharlal Nehru University, New Delhi. She was elected General President of the Indian History Congress in 1983, and is a Fellow of the British Academy. In 2008, she was awarded the prestigious Kluge Prize of the US Library of Congress, which honours lifetime achievements in studies such as History that are not covered by the Nobel Prize.

Michael Witzel studied at Tübingen and Erlangen Universities under Paul Thieme and Karl Hoffmann, completed his PhD in 1972 on the Katha Aranyaka, and studied Mimamsa at Kathmandu under Gurujyu Junanath Pandit. He taught at Tübingen (1972); from 1972–77, he was local director of the Nepal-German Manuscript Preservation Project at Kathmandu and of the Nepal Research Center; and from 1978–86, he was Professor of Sanskrit, Old and Middle Iranian at Leiden University. He has been Wales Professor of Sanskrit, Harvard University, since 1986. He is Editor of the Harvard Oriental Series, *Electronic Journal of Vedic Studies* and *Comparative Mythology*. He is President of the Association for the Study of Language in Prehistory and the International Association for Comparative Mythology.

Jaya Menon teaches archaeology in the Department of History at Shiv Nadar University. She has co-directed excavations at Indor Khera in Bulandshahr District and Rohana Khurd in Muzaffarnagar District in Uttar Pradesh. She has written on the archaeology of craft, childhood, households, and domestic space.

Kai Friese is a managing editor at *India Today* magazine.

Razib Khan is a geneticist who has contributed to *The Guardian, New York Times, India Today, National Review Online* and *Slate* on a broad range of topics. He has worked within the personal genomics industry for the past five years, and consults for PBS's *Finding Your Roots.*

BIBLIOGRAPHY & FURTHER READING

FOREWORD

Evans-Pritchard, E. E., *The Nuer*, Oxford: Clarendon Press, 1940; Nuer Religion, Oxford: Clarendon Press, 1956.

Kosambi, D. D., *The Culture and Civilisation of Ancient India in its Historical Outline*, London: Oxford University Press, 1965.

Lincoln, B., *Priests, Warriors and Cattle*, Berkeley: University of California Press, 1980.

BEYOND THE FLIGHT OF THE FALCON

Agrawal, D. P., *Central Himalayas: An Archaeological, Linguistic and Cultural Synthesis,* (with J. S. Kharakwal), New Delhi: Aryan Books International, 1998.

Andronov, Mikhail S., 'Comparative Studies on the Nature of Dravidian-Uralic Parallels: A Peep into the Prehistory of Language Families', *Proceedings of the Second International Conference of Tamil Studies,* Madras: International Association of Tamil Research, 1971.

Anthony, D. and D. Brown, 'The Dogs of War: A Bronze Age initiation ritual in the Russian steppe', *Journal of Anthropological Archaeology* 48, December 2017.

————, A. A. Khokhlov, P. F. Kuznetsov, O. D. Mochalov, *A Bronze Age Landscape in the Russian Steppes: The Samara Valley Project*, Los Angeles: Cotsen Institute of Archaeology, 2016.

Bal, Hartosh Singh, 'Indus Valley people did not have genetic contribution from the steppes: Head of Ancient DNA Lab testing Rakhigarhi samples', *Caravan*, 27 April 2018.

Balkan, K., *Kassitenstudien I. Die Sprache der Kassiten,* New Haven: American Oriental Society, 1954.

Bhutia, Lhendup G, 'The Genetic History of Indians: Are We What We Think We Are?', *Open* magazine, 20 April 2018.

Blazek, Vaclav, 'Was there an Australian Substratum in Dravidian?', *Mother Tongue,* XII, 2006.

Bopp, Franz, *Uber das conjugationsystem der Sanskritsprache,* Frankfurt: Andreaischen, 1816.

Buddruss, G., 'Zur Mythologie der Prasun-Kafiren', *Paideuma,* 7, 1960.

————, 'Vom mythischen Weltbild eines Hochgebirgsvolkes im Hindukush', in D. Zeller ed., *Religion und Weltbild,* Marburger Religionsgeschichtliche Beitrage2, (Munster: LIT), 2002.

————, 'Materialien zur Prasun-Sprache des Afghanischen Hindukusch, Teil I & II, Cambridge: Harvard Oriental Series, 2015–17.

Burrow, T., *Collected papers on Dravidian linguistics,* Annamalai: Annamalai University, 1968.

————, 'The Proto-Indo–Aryans', *Journal of the Royal Asiatic Society of Great Britain and Ireland,* No.2, 1973, pp. 123–40.

Caldwell, Robert, *A Comparative Grammar of the Dravidian or Indian Family of Languages,* London: Trubner, 1856.

Cavalli-Sforza, L.L., et al, *The History and Geography of Human Genes,* Princeton: Princeton University Press, 1994.

Diakonoff, I. M., *Hurrisch und Urartäisch,* Munchen: Kitzinger, 1971.

Ellis, Francis Whyte, 'Note to the Introduction', in A. D. Campbell, ed., *A Grammar of the Teloogoo Language,* Madras: College Press, 1816.

Frachetti, Michael D., 'The Inner Asian Mountain Corridor', *Current Anthropology* 53, 2012, pp. 2–38.

Francfort, H. P., 'The Central Asian dimension of the symbolic system in Bactria and Margiana', *Antiquity* 68, 1994.

Haak, Wolfgang et al, 'Massive migration from the steppe is a source for Indo-European languages in Europe', bioRxiv, posted February 10, 2015, bioRxiv, doi: http://dx.doi.org/10.1101/013433.

Harvard Round Tables 1999-2010, (http://www.people.fas.harvard.edu/~witzel/mwpage.htm).

Hoffmann, K., *Aufsätze zur Indoiranistik,* in J. Narten ed. J. Narten, Vols. 1–2. Wiesbaden: L. Reichert Verlag, 1975–76.

Medrano, Kastalia, 'Ancient China: 100 Horse Skeletons Discovered in 2,400-Year-Old Burial Pit Next to Tomb of Lord', *Newsweek,* 8 November 2017.

Joseph, Tony, 'How genetics is settling the Aryan migration debate', *The Hindu,* 16 June 2017.

Kenoyer, J. M., *Ancient Cities of the Indus Valley Civilization,* Oxford: Oxford University Press/ American Institute of Pakistan Studies, 1998.

———, 'Cultures and Societies of the Indus Tradition in Historical Roots', in Romila Thapar ed., *The Making of the 'Aryan',* New Delhi: National Book Trust, 2006.

Khatayat et al, 'The Indian Monsoon Variability and Civilization Changes in the Indian Subcontinent', *Science Advances,* 3, 2017. D OI: 10.1126/sciadv.1701296.

Koivulehto, J., 'The earliest contacts between Indo-European and Uralic speakers in the light of lexical loans', in Chr. Carpelan et al. *Early contacts between Uralic and Indo-European: Linguistic and archaeological considerations,* Helsinki: Suomalai–Ugrilainen Seura, 2001.

Krishnamurti, Bh., *The Dravidian Languages,* Cambridge: Cambridge University Press, 2003.

Kuiper, F. B. J., *Aryans in the Rigveda,* Amsterdam-Atlanta: Rodopi, 1991.

Kuz'mina, E., *The origin of the Indo-Iranians,* Leiden: Brill, 2007.

Laziridis, I., 'Massive migration from the steppe was a source for Indo-European languages in Europe', *Nature,* 522 (7555), 2015.

Lubotsky, A., 'The Indo-Iranian Substratum', in Chr. Carpelan et al., *Early Contacts between Uralic and Indo-European: Linguistic and Archaeological Considerations,* Helsinki: Suomalais-Ugrilainen Seura, 2001.

Magee, P., F. Khan, J. R. Knox, C. A. Petrie, and K. D. Thomas, 'Exploring Iron Age complexity in the North West Frontier Province, Pakistan: The 2000 season of excavations at Akra by the Bannu archaeological project', in C. Jarrige and V. Lefevre eds., *South Asian Archaeology 2001: Proceedings of the Sixteenth International Conference on South Asian Archaeology, European Association of South Asian Archaeologists,* Paris: Editions Recherche sur les Civilisations, Vol.1, 2005.

Mayrhofer, Manfred, *Die Arier im vorderen Orient–ein Mythos?* Vienna: Sitzungsberichte der Österreichischen Akademie der Wissenschaften, phil.-hist. Kl 294/3, 1974.

————, *Etymologisches Wörterbuch des Altindoarischen,* Heidelberg: C. Winter, 1986-2001.

McAlpin, David W., 'Elamite and Dravidian: Further evidence of relationship (with discussion by M. B. Emeneau, W. H. Jacobsen, F. B. J. Kuiper, H. H. Paper, E. Reiner, R. Stopa, F. Vallat, R. W. Wescott and a reply by McAlpin), *Current Anthropology,* 16, 1975.

————, *Proto-Elamian-Dravidian: The Evidence and its Implications.* Philadelphia: Transactions of the American Philosophical Society, 71, 1981.

Meadow, R. 'The Equids of Mehrgarh, Sibri and Pirak: An Osteological Evidence for the Introduction of the Horse to South Asia', Paper presented at the Seventh Conference of South Asian Archaeology, Brussels, 4–8 July 1983.

————, and A. Patel, 'A Comment on Horse Remains from Surkotada by Sandor Bokonyi, *South Asian Studies,* 13, 1997.

Moorjani, P., 'Genetic Evidence for Recent Population Mixture in India', *American Journal of Human Genetics*, Vol. 93 (3), 2013, pp. 422–38. <https://www.ncbi.nlm.nih.gov/pmc/articles/PMC3769933>

Narasimhan, V. M., et al., 'The Genomic Formation of South and Central Asia', bioRxiv: doi: https://doi.org/10.1101/292581, 2018.

Osada, Toshiki, A. Uesugi and M. K. V. Shinde, *Harappan Necropolis at Farmana in the Ghaggar Basin*, New Delhi: Indian Archaeological Society, 2009.

Parpola, Asko, *Deciphering the Indus Script,* Cambridge: Cambridge University Press, 1994.

Pitchappan, Ramsamy [on Australian genes in Tamil Nadu]: Zia Haq, 'Geneticists identify first Indians', *Hindustan Times*, 2 April 2008.

Pitch'jappan et al., 'Aboriginal Australian Mitochondrial Genome Variation: An Increased Understanding of Population Antiquity and Aiversity', doi: 10.1038/srep43041

Possehl, G. and P. Gullapalli, 'The Early Iron Age in South Asia', in V. Pigott ed., *The Archaeometallurgy of the Asian Old World,* Philadelphia: The University Museum, 1999, pp. 153–75.

Puhvel, J., *Comparative Mythology*, Baltimore and London: The Johns Hopkins University Press, 1987.

Raghu Vira and Lokesh Chandra, eds., *Jaiminiya Brahmana*, Nagpur: Sarasvati Vihar, 1954.

Rédei, K., *Zu den indogermanisch-uralischen Sprachkontakten.* Wien, Sitzungsberichte der Oesterreichischen Akademie der Wissenschaften, Philosophisch-Historische Klasse, 468 Band, 1986.

———, Die ältesten indogermanischen Lehnwörter der uralischen Sprachen, in: D. Sinor, ed., *The Uralic Languages: Description, History and Foreign influences.* Leiden: Brill, 1988: pp. 638–64.

Reich, D., et al., 'Reconstructing Indian population history', *Nature,* Volume 461, 24 September 2009, doi:10.1037/nature038365 https://www.nature.com/articles/nature08365.

SARVA Dictionary at ILCAA/TUFS, http://www.aa.tufs.ac.jp/ sarva/

Southworth, F. C., *Linguistic Archaeology of South Asia,* London and New York: Routledge, 2005.

———, 'New light on three South Asian language families', *Mother Tongue,* XI, 2006.

Srinivasan, D., 'Unhinging Siva from the Indus Civilization', *Journal of the Royal Asiatic Society of Great Britain and Ireland,* 1984.

Thapar, Romila, *The Past Before Us: Historical Traditions of Early North India,* New Delhi: Permanent Black, 2013.

Underhill, P, 'The Phylogenetic and Geographic Structure of Y-chromosome Haplogroup R1a', *European Journal of Human Genetics,* Vol. 23 (1), January 2015.

Valentine, B. *et al.*, 'Evidence for Patterns of Selective Urban Migration in the Greater Indus Valley (2600-1900 BC): A Lead and Strontium Isotope Mortuary Analysis', PLoS ONE, Vol. 10

(4), 29 April 2015.

Venkataramakrishnan, R., 'Do Rakhigarhi DNA findings debunk the Aryan invasion theory or give it more credence?', Scroll. in, 13 June, 2018.

Ventris, Michael, 'Function and Arabesque', *Plan: The Journal of the Architectural Students' Association,* 1948.

Vishnoi, Anubhuti, 'Harappan site of Rakhigarhi: DNA study finds no Central Asian trace, junks Aryan invasion theory', *Economic Times,* 13 June 2018.

Witzel, Michael, 'Early Sources for South Asian Substrate Languages', *Mother Tongue,* (Special Issue), October 1999.

———, 'The Home of the Aryans', in A. Hintze and E. Tichy eds. Anusantatyai. Fs. für Johanna Narten zum 70. Geburtstag, (Münchener Studien zur Sprachwissenschaft, Beihefte NF 19), Dettelbach: J.H. Roell 2000.

———, 'Autochthonous Aryans? The Evidence from Old Indian and Iranian Texts, *EJVS* 7-3, 25 May 2001.

———, 'Linguistic Evidence for Cultural Exchange in Prehistoric Western Central Asia', Philadelphia: *Sino-Platonic Papers* 129, 2003.

———, 'The Rigvedic Religious System and its Central Asian and Hindukush Antecedents', in A. Griffiths and J. E. M. Houben, eds., *The Vedas: Texts, Language and Ritual,* Groningen: Forsten, 2004.

———, 'Indocentrism: Autochthonous Visions of Ancient India', in Edwin F. Bryant and Laurie L. Patton, eds., *The Indo–Aryan Controversy: Evidence and Inference in Indian History,* London, New York: Routledge, 2005.

———, 'Vala and Iwato: The Myth of the Hidden Sun in India, Japan and Beyond, *EJVS, 12-1* (1 March 2005).

———, 'South Asian Agricultural Vocabulary', in T. Osada,

ed., *Proceedings of the Pre-Symposium of RHIN and 7th ESCA Harvard-Kyoto Round Table.* Research Institute for Humanity and Nature (RHIN), Kyoto 2006.

————, *The Origins of the World's Mythologies,* New York: Oxford University Press, 2012.

————, 'Mittani Indo–Aryan *Mazda* and the Date of the *Rigveda*', in D. N. Jha ed., *The Complex Heritage of Early India: Essays in Memory of R. S. Sharma,* Delhi: Manohar, 2014.

————, 'The Central Asian substrate in Old Iranian', *Mother Tongue* XX, 2015.

Zvelebil, K., *Comparative Dravidian Phonology,* The Hague: Mouton, 1970.

————, 'The descent of the Dravidians', *International Journal of Dravidian Linguistics* 1–2, 1972, pp. 56–63.

————, *Dravidian Linguistics: An Introduction,* Pondicherry: Pondicherry Institute of Linguistics, 1990.

MULTIPLE THEORIES ABOUT THE 'ARYAN'

Allchin, F. R., ed., *The Archaeology of Early Historic South Asia,* Cambridge: Cambridge University Press, 1995.

Anthony, D., 'Current Thoughts on the Domestication of the Horse in Asia', *South Asian Studies, Vol.13,* 1997.

Anthony, D. and D. Brown, 'The Origins of Horseback Riding', *Antiquity,* Volume 65, Issue 24, 6 March 1991.

Bryant, E., *The Quest for the Origins of Vedic Culture,* New Delhi: Oxford University Press, 2001.

Balibar, E., and Wallerstein I., *Race, Nation, Class,* London: Verso, 1991.

Bokonyi, S., 'Horse remains from the Prehistoric site of Surkotada,

Kutch, late 3rd Millennium BC', *South Asian Studies, Vol. 13*, 1997.

Bose, N. K., 'Caste in India', *Man in India*, 1951.

Bronkhorst, J. and M. M. Deshpande, eds., *Aryan and non-Aryan in South Asia*, Cambridge: Cambridge University Press, 1999.

Burrow, T., 'Iranian *arya* and *daha*', *Transactions of the Philological Society*, 1959.

————, 'The Proto-Indo–Aryans', *Journal of the Royal Asiatic Society, Vol. 2*, 1973.

————, *The Sanskrit Language*, London: Faber and Faber, 1965.

Caldwell, R., *A Comparative Grammar of the Dravidian or South Indian Family of Languages*, London: London: Trubner & Co, Ludgate Hill, 1856.

Chakrabarti, D. K., *The Archaeology of Ancient Indian Cities*, Delhi: Oxford University Press, 1995.

Darmesteter J., trs., *The Zend-Avesta, Part I The Vendidad*, Oxford: Clarendon Press, 1883.

Das, A. C., *Rigvedic India*, Calcutta: University of Calcutta, 1920.

Das, R. P., 'The Hunt for Foreign Words in the Rigveda', *Indo-Iranian Journal, Vol. 38*, 1995.

Deshpande, G. P., ed., *Selected Writings of Jotirao Phule*, Delhi: Manohar, 2002.

Deshpande, M. M., 'Genesis of Rigvedic Retroflexion', in M. M. Deshpande and P. Hook (eds.), *Aryan and Non-Aryan in India*, Ann Arbor: University of Michigan, Centre for South and Southeast Asian Studies, 1979.

Deo, S. B. and Kamath S., eds., *The Aryan Problem*, Pune: Bharatiya Itihasa Sankalana Samiti, 1993.

Drew, J., *India and the Romantic Imagination*, New Delhi: Oxford University Press, 1987.

Elliot, H. M. and Dowson J., *The History of India as Told by its*

Own Historians, London: Trubner & Co., 1869.

Ellis, P. W., 1816, 'Note to the Introduction', included in A. D. Campbell, *A Grammar of the Teloogoo Language*, quoted in part in T. Trautmann, ed., *The Aryan Debate*, New Delhi: Oxford University Press, 2005.

Emeneau, M. B., 'Linguistic Prehistory of India', in *Proceedings of the American Philosophical Society*, 98, 1954.

———, 'Indian Linguistic Area Revisited', *International Journal of Dravidian Linguistics*, 1974.

Erdosy, G., ed., *The Indo–Aryans of Ancient South Asia: Language, Material Culture and Ethnicity*, New York: De Gruyter, 1995.

Francfort, H-P., 'La civilisation de l'Oxus et les Indo-Iraniens et Indo-Aryens', in G. Pussman et at. (eds), *Aryas, Aryens et Iraniens en Asie Centrale*, Paris: Institut Civilisation Indienne, 2005.

Frawley, D., *The Myth of the Aryan Invasion of India*, New Delhi: Aditya Prakashan, 1994.

Fussman, G., 'Entre fantasmes, science et politique: l'entree des Aryas en Inde', in G. Fussman et al. (eds.), *Aryas, Aryens et Iraniens en Asie Centrale*, Paris: Institut Civilisation Indienne, 2005.

Ghurye, G. S., *Vedic India*, Delhi: Popular Prakashan, 1979.

Gimbutas, M., *The Kurgan Culture and the Indo-Europeanization of Europe*, Washington DC: Institute for the Study of Man, 1997.

Golwalkar, M. S., *We, Or Our Nationhood Defined*, Nagpur: Bharat Publications, 1938.

Goodrick-Clarke, N., *The Occult Roots of Nazism*, New York: I. B. Tauris, 1992.

Gordon, Childe V. G., *New Light on the Most Ancient East*, London: Kegan Paul, Trench, Trubner & Co., Ltd, 1934.

———, *The Aryans*, London: Kegan Paul, Trench, Trubner & Co., Ltd, 1926.

Gupta, S. P., 'Longer Chronology of the Indus Sarasvati Civilisation', *Puratattva*, 1992–93, 23.

Hiebert, P. T., *Origins of the Bronze Age Oasis Civilisation in Central Asia*, Cambridge, Massachusetts: Harvard University Press, 1994.

Hock, H. H., 'Whose past is it? Linguistic Pre- and Early History and Self-identification in Modern South Asia', *Studies in the Linguistic Sciences*, 2000.

——, 'Pre-Rigvedic convergence between Indo–Aryan (Sanskrit) and Dravidian? A Survey of the Issues and Controversies' in J. E. M. Houben, ed., *Ideology and Status of Sanskrit*, Leiden: Leiden University Press, 1996.

Hock, H. H., 'Subversion or Convergence? The Issue of Pre-Vedic Retroflexion Reexamined', in *Studies in the Linguistic Sciences*, 1993.

Ilaiah, K., *Why I am not a Hindu*, Calcutta: Bhatkal & Sen, 1996.

Jacobi, H., 'On the Date of the Rig-Veda', *Indian Antiquary*, 23, 1895.

Jarrige J-F. and M. Santoni, *Fouilles de Pirak*, Paris: Publications de la Commission des Fouilles Archéologique, 1979.

——, ed., *Les Cites oubliees de l'Indus*, Paris: Publications de la Commission des Fouilles Archéologique, 1988.

Jones, W., 1788, 'Third Anniversary Discourse', *Asiatic Researches*, 1, 415–31.

Karve, I., *Kinship Organisation in India*, Delhi: Munshiram Manoharlal, 1961.

Kellens, J., 'Les *airiia*-ne sont pas des Aryas: ce sont deja des Iraniens', in G. Fussman et al., eds., *Aryas, Aryens et Iraniens en Asie Centrale*, Paris: Publications de la Commission des Fouilles Archéologique, 2005.

Kenoyer, J. M., *Ancient Cities of the Indus Valley Civilization*, Karachi: Oxford University Press, 1988.

Kosambi, D. D., 'On the Origin of Brahmin Gotras', 1950, reprinted in ed. Brajadulal Chattopadhyaya *The Oxford India Kosambi: Combined Methods in Indology and Other writings*, New Delhi: Oxford University Press, 2002.

Kuiper, F. B. J., *Aryans in the Rigveda*, Amsterdam: Editions Rodopi B. V., 1991.

Agarwal, R. C., Lal, B. B., eds., *The Earliest Civilization of South Asia*, Delhi: Aryan Books International, 1997.

Leach, E., 'Aryan Invasions over Four Millennia', in E. Ohnuki-Tierney, ed., *Culture Through Time: Anthropological Approaches*, Stanford: Stanford University Press, 1990.

Leopold, J., 1974, 'British Applications of the Aryan Theory of Race to India, 1850–70', *The English Historical Review*, 89, 578–603; 'The Aryan Theory of Race in India 1870–1920, Nationalist and Internationalist Visions', *Indian Economic and Social History Review*, 1970, VII, 2.

Leslie Willson, A., *A Mythical Image: The Ideal of India in German Romanticism*, Durham: Duke University Press, 1964.

Lucas, J. R., ed., *The People of South Asia: The Biological Anthropology of India, Pakistan and Nepal*, New York: Springer, 1984.

Meadow, R. H., ed., *Harappa Excavations 1986-90. A Multi-Disciplinary Approach to Third Millennium Urbanism*, Madison: Prehistory Press, 1991.

Meadow, R. H. and Ajita Patel, 'A Comment on Horse Remains from Surkotada by Sandor Bokonyi', *South Asian Studies*, 1997.

Misra, V. N., 'Indus Civilisation and the Rigvedic Sarasvati', in A. Parpola et al., *South Asian Archaeology* 1993, Vol. II, Helsinki, 1994.

Majumdar, R. C., et al. (eds.), *The Vedic Age*, Bombay: Bharatiya Vidya Bhavan, 1951.

Mallory, J. P., *In Search of the Indo-Europeans*, London: Thames & Hudson, 1989.

Max Müller, F., *Lectures on the Science of Language*, London: Longmans, Greens & Co, 1862.

———, *India What Can it Teach Us?* London: Longmans, Greens & Co, 1883.

———, *Biographical Essays*, London: Longmans, Green & Co., 1884. [This was an address delivered at the Bristol Museum on 27.9.1883, on the 50th anniversary of the Raja's death. See also, N. Mookerjee, ed., *I Point to India*, Bombay 1970.]

———*Biographies of Words and the Home of the Aryas*, London: Longmans, Greens & Co, 1888.

———, ed., *Rigveda Samhita*, London: Trubner & Co., 1869.

———, *Auld Lang Syne*, New York: Charles Scribner's Sons, 1898.

———, *Chips from a German Workshop*, London: Longmans, Greens & Co, 1898.

Mehendale, M. A., 'Indo–Aryans, Indo-Iranians and Indo-Europeans', in S. B. Deo and S. Kamath (eds.), *The Aryan Problem*, Pune: Bharatiya Itihasa Sankalana Samiti, 1993.

Mughal, M. R., *Ancient Cholistan: Archaeology and Architecture*, Lahore: Ferozesons, 1997.

Muir, J., *Original Sanskrit Texts on the Origin and History of the People of India, Their Religion and Institutions*, London: Trubner & Co., 1874–84.

Nanda, M., *Prophets Facing Backwards: Postmodernism, Science, and Hindu Nationalism*, New Delhi: Permanent Black, 2003.

Narahari Achar B. N., 'On Exploring the Vedic Sky with Modern Computer Software', *Electronic Journal of Vedic Studies*, 5, 2, 1999.

O'Hanlon, R., *Caste Conflict and Ideology*, Cambridge: Cambridge University Press, 1985.

Omvedt, G., *Jyotiba Phule: An Incomplete Renaissance*, Surat, 1991.

Parpola, A., *Deciphering the Indus Script*, Cambridge: Cambridge University Press, 1994.

————, 'The Coining of the Aryans to Iran and India and the Cultural and Ethnic Identity of the Dasas', *Studia Orientalia*, 1988.

Phule J., *Gulamgiri*, 1873, Bombay 1986, tr., See also, G. P. Deshpande, ed., *Selected Works of Jyotirao Phule*, Delhi, 2002.

Poliakov, Léon, *The Aryan Myth: A History of Racist and Nationalist Ideas in Europe*, trs., Edmund Howard, New York: Basic Books. 1974.

Possehl, G., ed., *Harappan Civilization: A Recent Perspective*, New Delhi: American Institute of Indian Studies and Oxford & IBH Publication, 1993 (revised edition).

Rajaram, N. S., 'Vedic and Harappan Culture: New Findings', Puratattva, 1993–94.

————, *The Politics of History: Aryan Invasion theory and the Subversion of Scholarship*, New Delhi: Oxford University Press, 1995.

Ramaswamy, S., *Passions of the Tongue*, Berkeley: University of California Press, 1997.

Ratnagar, S., *Encounters: The Westerly Trade of the Harappan Civilisation*, New Delhi: Oxford University Press, 1981.

————, *Enquiries into the Political Organisation of Harappan Society*, Pune: Ravish Publishers, 1991.

————, *The End of the Great Harappan Tradition*, Delhi: Manohar, 2000.

Raulwing, P., *Horses, Chariots and Indo-Europeans*, Budapest: Archaeolingua, 2000.

Reich, David, *Who We are and How We got Here*, New York: Oxford University Press, 2018.

Renfrew, C., *Archaeology and Language: The Puzzle of Indo-European Origins*, Cambridge: Cambridge University Press, 1987.

Risley, H. H., *The People of India*, London: W. Thacker & Co, 1908.

Roy, T. N., *The Ganges Civilisation*, New Delhi: Ramanand Vidya Bhawan, 1983.

Sarianidi, V. I., 'Near Eastern Aryans in Central Asia', *The Journal of Indo-European Studies*, 27, 1999.

Savarkar, V. D., *Hindutva: Who is a Hindu?*, Bombay: Veer Savarkar Prakashan, 1922.

Schwab, R., trs., Gene Patterson-Black and Victor Reinking, *The Oriental Renaissance: Europe's Rediscovery of India and the East, 1680-1880*, New York: Columbia University Press, 1984.

Scott Littleton, C., *The New Comparative Mythology: An Anthropological Assessment of the Theories of Georges Dumézil*, Berkeley: University of California Press, 1973.

Sen, K. C., *Keshub Chunder Sen's Lectures in India*, London: Cassell and Company, Limited, 1904.

Sharma, R. S., *Advent of the Aryans in India*, Delhi: Manohar, 2001.

Staal, J. F., ed., *Agni: The Vedic Ritual of the Fire Altar*, Berkeley: University of California Press, 1983.

Stepan, Nancy, *The Idea of Race in Science: Great Britain 1800-1960*, London: Palgrave Macmillan, 1982.

Talageri, S., *Aryan Invasion Theory and Indian Nationalism*, New Delhi: Voice of India, 1993.

Taylor, I., *The Origin of the Aryans: An Account of the Prehistoric Ethnology and Civilisation of Europe*, London: Walter Scott Ltd, 1889.

Thapar, R., 1969, 'Society in Ancient India: the Formative Period', reprinted in R.Thapar, *Cultural Pasts: Essays in Early Indian History*, New Delhi: Oxford University Press, 2000.

————, 'Origin Myths and the Early Indian Historical Tradition', 1978, reprinted in R. Thapar, *Cultural Pasts*, New Delhi: Oxford University Press, 2000, pp. 754-781.

————, 'The Archaeological Background to the Agnicayana Ritual', in F. Staal et al., eds., *Agni*, Berkeley: University of California Press, 1983.

————, *From Lineage to State*, New Delhi: Oxford University Press, 1984.

————, 'Archaeology and Language at the Roots of Ancient India', *Journal of the Asiatic Society of Bombay*, 64-66 (n.s.), 1989–91.

————, '*Rigveda*: Encapsulating Social Change', in K. N. Panikkar et al. (eds.), *The Making of History*, Delhi: Manohar, 2000.

————, Thapar, R. et al., *India: Historical Beginnings and the Concept of the Aryan*, New Delhi: National Book Trust, 2006.

Tilak, B. G., *Orion or Researches into the Antiquity of the Vedas*, Bombay: Mrs Radhabai Atmaram Sagoon, 1893.

————, *The Arctic Home in the Vedas*, Poona: Messrs, Tilak Bros, 1903

Trautmann, T. R., *Aryans and British India*, New Delhi: Oxford University Press, 1997.

————, ed., *The Aryan Debate*, New Delhi: Oxford University Press, 2005.

Waddell, L. A., *The Indo-Sumerian Seals Deciphered*, London: Luzac & Co., 1925.

Wilson, J., *Indian Caste*, Bombay: Times of India Office, 1877.

Witzel, M., 'The Pleiades and the Bears Viewed from Inside the Vedic Texts', *Electronic Journal of Vedic Studies*, 5.2, 1999.

————, 'Tracing the Vedic Dialects', in C. Caillat, ed., *Dialectes dans les Litteratures Indo-Aryennes*, Paris: Paris de France/Institut de Civilisation Indienne, 1989.

————, ed., *Inside the Texts Beyond the Texts*, Cambridge, Massachusetts: Harvard University Press, 1997.

————, 'Autochthonous Aryans? The Evidence from Old Indian and Iranian texts', *Electronic Journal of Vedic Studies*, 2001.

IN THE AFTERMATH OF THE HARAPPAN PERIOD (*c.* 2000–500 BCE)

Allchin, B. and R. Allchin, *The Rise of Civilization in India and Pakistan*, New Delhi: Selectbook Service Syndicate, 1989 (reprint).

Allchin, R. and B. Allchin, *Origins of a Civilization: The Prehistory and Early Archaeology of South Asia*, New Delhi: Penguin Books, 1997.

Green, A. S. and C. A. Petrie, 'Landscapes of Urbanization and de-urbanization: A large-scale approach to investigating the Indus Civilization's settlement distributions in northwest India', *Journal of Field Archaeology* 43, pp. 4: 284–99, 2018, DOI: 10.1080/00934690.2018.1464332.

Hiebert, F. T., *Origins of the Bronze Age Civilization in Central Asia*, American School of Prehistoric Research Bulletin 42, Harvard: Peabody Museum of Archaeology and Ethnology, 1994.

Hemphill, Brian. E., John R. Lukacs and K. A. R. Kennedy, 'Biological adaptations and affinities of Bronze age Harappans', in Richard H. Meadow, ed., *Harappa Excavations, 1986-1990*, Madison: Prehistory Press, 1991, pp. 137–82.

Joshi, J. P., *Excavation at Bhagwanpura 1975-76 and Other*

Explorations & Excavations 1975-81 in Haryana, Jammu & Kashmir and Punjab, New Delhi: Archaeological Survey of India, 1993.

Madella, M. and D. Q. Fuller, 'Palaeoecology and the Harappan Civilization of South Asia: A reconsideration', *Quaternary Science Reviews* 25: 1283-1301, 2006.

Menon, J. and S. Varma, 'Defining Tradition: An Archaeological Perspective', in S. Sabharwal and S. Varma, eds., *Traditions in Motion: Religion and Society in History*, New Delhi: Oxford University Press, 2005, pp. 23–49.

Mughal, M. R., *Ancient Cholistan: Archaeology and Architecture*, Lahore: Ferozesons (Pvt.) Ltd, 1997.

Reich, David, *Who We Are and How We got Here*, New York: Pantheon Books, 2018.

Possehl, G. L., *The Indus Civilization: A Contemporary Perspective*, New Delhi: Vistaar, 2002.

Ratnagar, S., *The End of the Great Harappan Tradition*, New Delhi: Manohar, 2000.

Shaffer, J. G. and D. A. Lichtenstein, 'Ethnicity and change in the Indus Valley cultural tradition', in J.M. Kenoyer ed., *Old Problems and New Perspectives in the Archaeology of South Asia*, Madison: Wisconsin Archaeological Reports, Vol. 2, 1989, pp. 117–26.

Sharma, D. V., K. C. Nauriyal, V. N. Prabhakar and Vishnukant, 'Sanauli: A late Harappan burial site in the Yamuna-Hindon Doab', *Puratattva* 34: 35-44, 2003–04.

Sharma, D. V., K. C. Nauriyal and V. N. Prabhakar, 'Excavations at Sanauli 2005–06: A Harappan necropolis in the upper Ganga-Yamuna Doab', *Puratattva* 36: 166-179, 2005–06.

Varma, S., 'In the absence of mounds: Shifting villages, pastoralism and depopulation', in R. C. Heredia and S. F. Ratnagar, eds.,

Mobile and Marginalized Peoples: Perspectives from the Past, Delhi: Manohar, 2003, pp. 121–44.

Wright, R., *The Ancient Indus: Urbanism, Economy, and Society*, Cambridge: Cambridge University Press, 2010.

AFTERWORD

Aitareya Brahmana, in A. B. Keith, *Rigveda Brahmanas,* Cambridge, Massachusetts: Harvard University Press, 1920.

Bronkhorst, J and M. M. Deshpande (eds.), *Aryan and non-Aryan in South Asia: Evidence, Interpretation and Ideology,* Cambridge, Massachusetts: Harvard University Press, 1999.

Bryant E., *The Quest for the Origins of Vedic Culture*, New Delhi: Oxford University Press, 2014.

Brhad-devata, M. Tokunaga, ed., Kyoto: Rinsen, 1997.

Chhandogya Upanisad, in S. Radhakrishnan, ed., *The Principal Upanisads,* London: George Allen & Unwin, 1953.

Dandekar, R. N., *Vedic Mythological Tracts*, Delhi: Ajanta Publications, 1979.

———, 'Vedic Mythology: A Rethinking', in M. Witzel, *Inside the Texts Beyond the Texts*, Cambridge, Massachusetts: Harvard University Press, 1997.

Deshpande, M. M.,, 'Socio-Linguistics Attitudes in India', *Linguistica Extranea*, Series 5, Ann Arbor: University of Michigan Press, 1979.

———, ed., *Aryan and non-Aryan in South Asia,* Cambridge, Massachusetts: Harvard University Press, 1999.

———,'What to do with the Anaryas?' in Bronkhorst and Deshpande, 1999.

Dhavalikar, M. D., *The Aryan Myth and Archaeology*, New Delhi: Munshiram Manoharlal, 2007.

Erdosy G., ed., *The Indo–Aryans of Ancient South Asia: Language, Material Culture and Ethnicity*, Berlin: De Gruyter, 1995.

Kausitaki Brahmana in A. B. Keith, *Rigveda Brahmanas*, Cambridge, Massachusetts: Harvard University Press, 1920.

Kuiper F. B. J., *Aryans in the Rigveda*, Amsterdam: Editions Rodopi B.V., 1991.

Lal, B. B., *The Homeland of the Aryans: Evidence of Rigvedic Flora and Archaeology*, New Delhi: Aryan Books International, 2005.

Mahadevan, I., 'The Unicorn and the Sacred Filter Standard', *International Journal of Dravidian Linguistics*, 46, 1, 2017.

Majjhima Nikaya, 1888-96, Pali Text Society, London

Malamoud, C., *Cooking the World*, New Delhi: Oxford University Press, 1976.

Mallory, J. P., *In Search of the Indo-Europeans. Language, Archaeology and Myth*, London: Thames & Hudson, 1989.

Ratnagar S., 'Does Archaeology Hold the Answer' in Bronkhorst, J and M. M. Deshpande (eds.), *Aryan and non-Aryan in South Asia: Evidence, Interpretation and Ideology*, Cambridge, Massachusetts: Harvard University Press, 1999.

———, 'The Aryan homeland debate in India', in P. L. Kohl, M. Kozelsky and N. Ben-Yehuda, eds., *Selective Remembrances: Archaeology in the Construction, Commemoration, and Consecration of National Pasts*, Chicago and London: Chicago University Press, 2007.

Reich, D., *Who We Are and How We Got Here: Ancient DNA and the New science of the Human past*, London: Oxford University Press, 2018.

Satapatha Brahmana, Delhi: Sacred Books of the East, 1972.

Sharma R. S., *Advent of the Aryans in India*, Delhi: Manohar, 2001.

Skjaervo, P. O., 'The Avesta as source for the Early History of

Iranians', in Bronkhorst and Deshpande.

Staal, F. ed., *Agni: The Vedic Ritual of the Fire Altar*, Berkeley: University of California Press, 1983.

———, *Discovering the Vedas*, New Delhi: Penguin Books, 2008.

Thapar, R., 1978, 'A Possible Identification of Meluhha, Dilmun and Makan' in R. Thapar, *Cultural Pasts*, New Delhi: Oxford University Press, 2000.

———, 'The Archaeological Background to the Agnicayana', in F. Staal, ed., *Agni*, 1983.

———, *The Aryan: Recasting Constructs*, Gurgaon: Three Essays Collective, 2008.

Trautmann, T. R., *Aryans and British India*, New Delhi: Oxford University Press, 1997.

———, *The Aryan Debate*, New Delhi: Oxford University Press, 2005.

Wasson, R. G., *Soma: Divine Mushroom of Immortality*, New York: Harcourt Brace Jovanovich, Inc., 1968.

Witzel, M., *Inside the Texts Beyond the Texts: New Approaches to the Study of the Vedas*, Cambridge, Massachusetts: Harvard University Press, 1997.

———, 'Early Indian History: Linguistic and Textual Parameters', in G. Erdosy, 1997.

INDEX

'Ancestral North Indians' (ANI), 17, 113, 128
'Ancestral South Indians' (ASI), 17, 113, 128
Achaemenid, 162
Ahura Mazda, 71
Airiia, vii, 40, 65, 71, 159
Ajivikas, 77
aṃśu, 12
Anarya, 162, 163
Anatolia, xiv, 9, 31, 60, 64, 74, 75, 160
Andronovo culture, 10
Aushija, Kakshivant, 165
Aranyakas, xi
Archaeological Survey of India, 128
Ariya Dhamma, 163
Arya, vii, viii, 2, 4, 25, 28, 35, 40, 44, 46, 48, 49, 53, 65, 75, 76, 81, 87, 92, 159, 161, 162, 163, 164, 165, 171
Arya Samaj, 52, 53
Arya varna, 44, 163,
Aryan Brahmana, 81
Aryan Invasion theory, 121, 125, 126
Arya-putra, 162
Aryavak, 2

Aryavarta, 4, 27, 163, 168
Asura/Ahura, 10, 65
Atharvaveda, 11, 15
Avesta, 26, 31, 40, 65, 66, 68, 71, 72, 75

Bactria–Margiana Archaeological Complex (BMAC), 12, 69
Balbutha, 14, 21, 28, 76, 172
Bali, 49
Black-and-Red-Ware (BRW), 109
Brahmana, 15, 48, 49, 52, 67, 76, 81, 163, 164, 165, 172
Brahmins, 20, 23, 27, 49, 125, 141, 142, 144, 152
Bribu, 14, 21, 28, 76, 172
Bronze Age, 5, 11, 20, 28, 95, 122, 129, 145, 147, 148, 149

Carvakas, 77
Caspian Sea, 65
Caste, viii, 18, 44, 47, 48, 50, 51, 52, 53, 54, 55, 56, 76, 77, 78, 81, 82, 83, 84, 124, 140, 141, 145, 150, 151, 153, 163
Cemetery H, 3, 99, 100, 101, 102, 103, 111

Central Asia, 174, 175
Chamar, 141
Chandala, 81
Childe, Gordon, 85
Cholistan, 87, 97, 100, 102, 104,
    110, 111, 112
Chota Nagpur plateau, 143
Contamination, 118, 129, 131,
    174
Copper Hoards, 99, 101, 117

Daitya, 49, 162
Darius, 2, 162
Dasa, 44, 46, 65, 76, 162, 163,
    164, 166, 172
Dasi, 67, 76, 164, 165
Dasi-putra Brahmana, 67, 164,
    172
Dasyus, 164
Dayanand Saraswati, 52, 82
Deadman Lane, 96
Dharmashastras, 76, 162, 163
DNA, 113, 114, 115, 119, 122–26,
    128, 130–32, 135, 136, 137,
    146, 147, 149, 150, 151, 153,
    154, 174, 175
Dravidian language, 15, 17, 38,
    45, 49, 114, 124
Dravidian race, 45

Equus caballus, 112

Gandhara Grave Culture, 6, 27,
    98
Ganga–Yamuna Doab, 99, 102,
    110

Gathas, 71
German Romanticism, 39, 41,
    54
Golwalkar, M. S., 81, 126
Greater Indus Valley, 99, 100,
    106, 111

Hakra River, 87, 112, 173
Han Chinese, 133
Harappan Civilization, 3, 4, 14,
    15, 17, 19, 27, 85, 95, 97,
    105, 119, 120
Harappan Period, 94, 96, 99, 100,
    101, 103, 106, 110, 148, 179
Hindu Rashtra, 81
Hindutva, 5, 8, 55, 79, 81, 87,
    88, 92, 120, 121, 126, 127,
    128, 131
horse burials, 98

Indo–Aryan, vii, xiv, xv, 1, 2, 3,
    5, 6–8, 9, 10, 11, 12–19, 20,
    21, 26, 27, 28, 31, 32, 38, 45,
    46, 50, 57, 63, 64–66, 68, 72,
    74, 75, 82, 88, 89, 90, 91,
    115, 146, 147, 151, 154, 159,
    160, 163, 166, 169, 172
Indo–European, viii, 5, 8, 9, 14,
    17, 21, 22, 23, 24, 26, 28, 31,
    38, 39, 40, 43, 59, 60, 66,
    70, 75
Indus Civilization, 10, 21, 22,
    23, 27, 30, 56, 57, 62, 85,
    87, 106, 112, 132
Indus–Hakra, 87
Indus–Sarasvati, 87

Inner Asian mountain corridor, 20, 26
Iranians, 2, 10, 140
Iron Age, 6, 28, 94, 97, 99, 109, 148
Iron Age communities, 97
Irula, 124, 132

Jacobi, Hermann, 67
Jati, 55, 83, 142, 143
Jats, 125, 141
Jhukar, 99, 100, 101, 108, 116

Kali Yuga, 5, 58
Kassites, 26, 27, 160
Kavasha Ailusha, 160, 165
Kaveri valley, 170
Krittika, 67
Kshatr, 74
Kshatriya, 4fn, 15, 24, 49

loanwords, 5, 7, 10, 11, 12, 13, 25, 26, 28, 165

Mahabharata, 58
Manu, 35, 168,
Mature Harappan, 4, 32, 87, 95, 96, 96fn, 97, 99, 100, 101, 102, 103–11, 116–18, 122, 148
Milakkhu, 16, 162
Mitanni–Hittite Treaty, 64, 75
Mitra, 11, 65
Mitra–Varuna, 171
Mleccha, vii, 16, 162, 163
Mohenjodaro, 56, 96, 116, 121, 134

mtDNA, 16, 17, 137, 138, 139, 140, 141, 144, 146, 148
Mūjavant Mountain, 12, 23
Müller, Max, 43, 44–46, 48, 50, 51, 59, 82

Narasimhan, Vageesh 18, 19, 20, 21, 115, 129, 130, 132
Nilgiri highlands, 124

Ochre Coloured Pottery (OCP), 99, 101, 102, 117
Oxus Civilization, 69

Painted Grey Ware (PGW), 4, 86, 89, 94, 99, 100
Panini, 39, 163, 169,
petrous bone, 17, 119
Phule, Jyotiba, 49, 50, 52, 81, 82, 83
Pirak, 13, 97
Pitribhumi, 55, 80
Pleiades, 67
Prakrit, 9, 89, 163,
Proto-Indo–Aryans, xiv, 15
Punyabhumi, 55, 80
Pur, 73
Pura, 73
Puranas, 34, 35, 46, 77

R1a, 174, 176
R1a1a, 144, 145, 146–48, 149, 150, 153
racial segregation, 47, 48, 83
Rai, Niraj, 19, 119, 122, 125
Rakhigarhi, 17, 18, 19, 27, 106,

115, 119, 121–26, 129, 130,
131, 133, 148, 150
Rakshasa, 162
Rangpur, 99, 100, 101
Reich, David, 17, 113, 114, 128,
129, 133
Rig Veda , 159, 160, 162, 163,
164, 165, 167, 170, 171, 173

Sabhas, 73
Samaveda, xi, 32, 33
samitis, 73
Sanskrit, ix, xiv, 2, 23, 27, 36,
37–39, 41, 43, 44, 48,
82, 88, 89, 90, 109, 112,
115–16, 119, 123, 158, 163,
173
Saptarishi, 67
Satyakama Jabala, 164
Savarkar, V. D., 80
Sayana, 43, 44, 58
Shakalya, 78, 160
Shastras, 52
Shinde, Vasant, 120, 121, 125,
129, 130
Shiva, 162,
Shramana, 77, 162
Shrauta-sutras, xi
Shudra, 15, 16, 28, 49, 171
Sindhu, 10, 71, 79, 173
Sindhusthan, 87
Siswal, 99, 100, 105, 107, 111
Sothi–Siswal, 100, 108
South Asian, 10, 114, 123, 140,
141, 142, 143, 144, 146, 148,
149, 154

steppe, 5, 10, 19, 20, 21, 25, 27,
29, 70, 114, 122, 123, 124,
125, 129, 132, 145, 148, 149,
150, 151, 152, 153, 154, 165,
175
substrate languages, 14, 133
Sutlej–Yamuna Divide, 99, 100,
103, 104, 108, 110, 111
Swat Valley, 18, 20, 86, 130, 148,
150, 152

Telugu, 37, 38
terracotta figurines, 98
Thar Desert, 102
Tilak, B. G., 49, 50, 82

Upanishads, xi

Vaishya, 15
Varuna, 11, 65
Vedic corpus, viii, xiv, 38, 56,
57, 62, 67, 68, 85, 88, 89,
92, 161, 164, 168, 171
Vidathas, 73
Vindhyas, x, 90, 121, 168
Vish, 74
Vrātyas, 24, 28

Wesolowski, David, 125, 126
West Asia, 31, 34, 64, 97, 124,
144, 148, 149

Yajurveda, xi, 32, 33
Y-chromosomal lineage, 140, 144,
147